Growing Pains

How to **S. L. A. Y.** Life's Giants in 31 Days

STEPHANIE L. RANDALL

Copyright © 2016 by Stephanie L. Randall
All rights reserved. This book or any portion thereof may not be reproduced or used in any manner whatsoever without the express written permission of the publisher except for the use of brief quotations in a book review.

Limits of Liability and Disclaimer of Warranty

The author and publisher shall not be liable for your misuse of this material. This book is strictly for informational and educational purposes. The purpose of this book is to educate and entertain. The author and/or publisher do not guarantee that anyone following these techniques, suggestions, tips, ideas, or strategies will become successful. The author and/or publisher shall have neither liability nor responsibility to anyone with respect to any loss or damage caused, or alleged to be caused, directly or indirectly by the information contained in this book. Scriptures taken directly from ESV.

Views expressed in this publication do not necessarily reflect the views of the publisher.

Cover design by Brittney Morton
Book design and production by Keen Vision Publishing
Author photograph by Ayanah George

Printed in the United States of America

ISBN: 978-0692744017

Keen Vision Publishing

This book is dedicated to my angels in Heaven. My maternal grandmother Virginia "Jenni" Arter. You will always be my light and my love. To my great aunt ,Yvonne Jean Short I will always remember our card games, movie nights and late night snacks of butter pecan ice cream. To my great aunt, Vivian Cunningham thank you for always leading by example and showing me what excellence looks like. I miss you all dearly and carry you in my heart. Rest peacefully until we are joined together again.

Acknowledgements

God has allowed my triumphs to be greater than my trials, and for that I am eternally grateful. For without Him there would be no me. I want to honor my mother, **BJ Smith**, for sacrificing, so much for me over the years. Your hard work has not gone unnoticed. You are the epitome of strength, and have shown me how to be more resilient.

To my amazing mentor, **Niyonu Greene**, words cannot express the gratitude I feel having you in my life. Your prayers, faith, and guidance have been invaluable. Thank you for always pouring into me, and uplifting me in the difficult times.

To two of my best friends, **Fatima Al-Amin-El and Jarra Childs**, thank you for being my A-one's, since day one! You have wiped so many tears, supported my business ventures, encouraged me through hard times and celebrated with me through the good ones. No matter what I need, you have given without hesitation. I am truly blessed to have such amazing friends that have become family.

Thank you to all my family members who have acted as great examples for me. **Rosa Thomas, David and Denise Arter, Larry and Maritza Carpenter,** and the countless others who have been there for me over the years.

Thank you to my **QE Ministry Queens**. I have experienced so much growth over the last three years participating and serving in the ministry. It has pushed me to be a better woman, and has been a major part of my healing process.

Thank you to my **Sorors** and **Visionary** for always keeping me lifted in prayer, loving me unconditionally and allowing me to be among such phenomenal women.

About the Author

Stephanie L. Randall is a native Washingtonian. She began writing short stories and poetry at the age of fifteen, in hopes of one day becoming a published author. Stephanie is an Alumna of the **University of Maryland Eastern Shore** where she studied hotel and restaurant management. She is the owner of **The Sunday Dinner Catering and Event Planning Service**, and the founder of **My Divine Opportunity, LLC**. Stephanie plays an active role in her community, as well as her church. She has a passion for mentoring and supporting young men and women, and continues to do so through her position as an adjunct professor.

Contents

INTRO 1
VICTIM OR VICTOR 1
A MOTHERLESS CHILD 5
FAMILY TIES 13
UNTIL WE MEET AGAIN 19
COUNT IT ALL JOY 25
RELEASE GUILT & SHAME 29
PRAY WITHOUT CEASING 35
EMOTIONAL ROLLERCOASTER 41
HOW DO YOU ENDURE? 47
NEGATIVE NANCY 53
LOWERED EXPECTATIONS 57
PEOPLE PLEASERS 63
WHAT ABOUT YOUR FRIENDS? 69
ANGER & ANIMOSITY 77
FIGHTING FEAR 83
CORPORATE AMERICA 89
ENVY IS YOUR ENEMY 97
DATING & WAITING 103
GUILTY BY ASSOCIATION 111
WE WEAR THE MASKS 119
ALONE & NOT LONELY 125
TUNNEL VISION 131
MARRIAGE IS THE MOTIVE 137
LOST IN LUST 145
TWO-FACED 149
HUMILITY & NOT HUMILIATION 153

KEEPING SECRETS & STEALING INNOCENCE	161
GOD, YOUR CREDIT IS GOOD WITH ME	169
RUN YOUR RACE	173
DON'T GET LOST IN THE LESSON	179
NOT BUILT TO BREAK	185

As we face the obstacles that life brings, our goal should be to evolve. Like the caterpillar who is destined to be a butterfly we go through Growing Pains in order for our true purpose to be birthed. We are stretched, tested, and put through many trials before we gain our wings and the strength to fly.

This 31 Day journey will teach you how to **S.L.A.Y.** the giants you will face in life. Remember, in order to overcome any obstacle you need to **S**eek God first, **L**et go of the past, **A**ccept what you cannot change, and **Y**ield to HIS will. It's time to **S.L.A.Y.** !

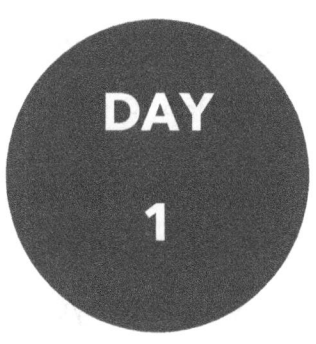

VICTIM OR VICTOR

"For the righteous falls seven times and rises again, but the wicked stumble in times of calamity." Proverbs 24:16 (ESV)

You have the choice to write your own story. It may not have begun as a fairytale, but it can still end with a happily ever after. You must choose. You cannot straddle the fence on being a victim or victor. A victor is a person who defeats an enemy or opponent in a battle, game, or other competition. It's okay to tell your story and shed your tears, but as a victor, you cannot hold on to the hurt. When we allow ourselves to become a victim, we forfeit the opportunity to bless and change the lives of others through our story. When we have a skewed vision of life, we run the risk of never experiencing what life truly has to offer.

Have you been hurt by people of your past? Did someone steal something more valuable than money from you? Has your family scarred you? Were you betrayed by so-called friends? If you answered yes to any of those questions, know that you can still be victorious. It's time to take control of your situation! You must decide to no longer consume yourself with the pain of yesterday, and move forward to the hope of tomorrow. Healing from your past does not come by luck. Instead, it requires a conscious decision. You must decide in your heart that you want to get through what is causing you pain. You must set your mind on moving past whatever is hindering you from living your best possible life. No, you will not automatically forget about everything that has transpired over the course of your life. God does not desire us to forget those things. He desires that we learn from those situations.

When I reminisce on some of my darker times, I gain perspective on how far I have come, and just how much more God is going to do for me and through me. It might sound crazy, but this perspective allows me to be grateful for everything I've experienced. I'm grateful because I've learned that there is purpose in our pain. When we understand that there is truly purpose in our pain, we can deal with life's obstacles a little better.

Do you want to live in favor or fear? God can grant you favor. Only God can turn your fear into faith, and your pain into purpose. All He requires is that you release your issues to Him. You have to decide what you want and how hard you are willing to work for it. Healing from pain takes work. When we refuse to work through our healing, we drag our baggage and hurt along every aspect of our life's journey. Our past pain then affects our existing relationships, friendships and view on life in general.

Are you ready to exchange your heartbreak for healing? Are you ready to trust again? Are you ready for relationships with the type of people you desire, rather than the type of people who hurt you? Are you ready to live the life you always dreamed of living? Are you ready to walk boldly in your purpose? I pray you answered yes to each of these questions. This devotional is designed not to help you get over your past, but to get through it. Within this devotional, you will find my experiences and life lessons. At the end of each day, there are self-reflecting questions to help you dig deep and heal at your very core. Be open. Be honest. Grab your journal and record your responses. Be sure to date your entries! In addition to the questions, you will find scriptures for meditation. I pray this devotional helps you to realize all that you are and all that you have yet to become!

Self-Reflection: Take a moment to answer the following questions.

- What area of your life have you felt like a victim?
- How can you change your circumstances and gain victory?

Suggested Scripture(s):

"Fear not, for I am with you; be not dismayed, for I am your God; I will strengthen you, I will help you, I will uphold you with my righteous right hand." Isaiah 41:10 (ESV)

Now these things happened to them as an example, but they were written down for our instruction, on whom the end of the ages has come." 1 Corinthians 10:11 (ESV)

DAY 2

A MOTHERLESS CHILD

"Can a woman forget her nursing child, that she should have no compassion on the son of her womb? Even these may forget, yet I will not forget you." Isaiah 49:15 (ESV)

I look just like my mother. I love her smile. It has always brought reassurance when I'm down or confused. She was always so comforting to me as a child. She called me her pumpkin, brushed my hair and always tucked me in at night. As I grew older, I saw how hardworking my mother was. She wanted the best things in life, however, happiness appeared elusive. For my mother, happiness was like an unobtainable goal that was always a few steps out of her reach. Don't get me wrong. She was happy and enjoyed her life, but she did not have joy.

The more she obtained, the more she needed. She has a void that nothing or no one could fill. She was beyond self-sufficient. The issue was that she was so self-sufficient, she didn't want anyone around. Sometimes, I believed she didn't even want me around. I desired to be wanted by her. I needed to know that I was her light in a dark situation. My mother was a great provider, but emotionally there was a void. The absence of my father came as no surprise to me. He was not a present or consistent figure in my life, and I was okay with that. However, having my mother physically present, yet emotionally absent was a hard pill to swallow.

My mother was one out of ten children. As a child, many of her wants and needs were placed on the back burner to help with her nine brothers and her sister. I took for granted that we always had a nice, clean, and spacious home. I was rarely appreciative that I had enough to eat, and was blessed to have everything I needed and some of my desires. I was "too emotional" for her, and she was too cold for me.

Now my grandmother, Jenni, on the other hand, was very different. She was nothing like these new age grandmothers who are too young to be bothered with babysitting their grandchildren. My grandmother was my comforter. My earliest memories of my grandmother were sitting around the dining room table playing deuces, trouble, and crazy 8s. To me, my grandmother was the greatest woman in the world after my mother. She spoiled me rotten and loved me as much as I loved her. Little did I know, my mother felt that the love I had for my grandmother overshadowed the love I had for her.

I was my mother's only child. I was all she had, but just like most children, I clung to my grandmother. I could not recognize how I hurt my mother by my actions. I unintentionally caused division between my mother and me. My love for my grandmother led her to focus on children who really needed her. My mother decided to become a foster parent. She wanted to help children whose parents were not able to take care of them. Being an only child, I was excited to have siblings around. We moved to Maryland into an attached three level three-bedroom townhouse.

When I met the first set of foster children, I wasn't sure what to think. They seemed to be friendly enough, but they also seemed to have baggage with them, and I don't just mean suitcases. Being a foster mother gave my mother a new sense of purpose. She loved feeling needed, which was a feeling I guess I was no longer able to convey to her.

Over the next several years we had foster children come and go. My mother poured into them and gave them the love they lacked. Having foster siblings caused me to grow up a lot sooner than I had planned. I had to learn how to fend for myself. When I was ten-years-old, my mother brought home a small baby, only a few weeks old. The little girl had been abandoned by her mother. She became the light of our lives. It was my mother's chance at a fresh start. She cared for this baby as if she was her own. She was no longer a motherless child.

By the time I was eighteen-years-old, I was working and living on my own. The time outside of my mother's household allowed us to actually grow closer. Over the years, our relationship was like a yo-yo pulling each other closer, and sometimes pushing each other away. As I got deeper into my relationship with God, He began to reveal some things to me about my relationship with my parents. Encountering children whose mothers had passed away, were abusive, drug addicts or just decided they no longer wanted to be a parent was an eye opener. I realized that I had on blinders for most of my childhood. I had expected my mother to be perfect like Clair Huxtable, while seldom realizing that she was only able to give what she had received.

I learned that my expectations and my reality were two totally different things. We had lived two different lifestyles, had seen different things, and had dealt with our feelings in ways that were difficult for one another to understand. My mother prided herself on her independence, which I had always admired and even aspired to achieve. She had created a home from her hard work and had overcome the statistics of growing up in S.E. DC. She had not been afforded the opportunities that I had and had dealt with her hardships and disappointments from her parents the best way she knew how.

God gave me compassion and understanding. In life, we sometimes struggle to give what we feel we have not received, not understanding that people communicate and express love differently. My mother showed her love by providing for me. She desired my love in return but was not quite sure how to receive it. I could see that she wanted to make an effort to give me what I needed as her child. We had to learn to meet each other half way. I prayed that God would touch the hearts of my parents so they could give me the peace that I needed to lead a healthy and happy life. I quickly learned that I would have to be okay if that never happened. In spite of everything, God has guided me and protected me my whole life. He has blessed me tremendously and allowed me to grow through the pain of my past.

One morning, I woke up out of my sleep at 5:30 am. I had not planned to be up for another few hours. I was unsure of why I was wide awake. I grabbed my cellphone and saw my email notifications. I scrolled through and saw an untitled email from my mom. I opened it and began to read the long, detailed email that gave me everything I wanted and even some of what

I did not know I needed. Tears of joy streamed down my cheeks, and I just shouted, "Thank You, Jesus!"

Growing Pains Life Lesson

That heartfelt letter gave me the peace, understanding, and information I needed to have a better understanding of my parents and what made them who they are. I am thankful that my mother is still here for me to continue to work on our relationship. I urge you to make amends and gain closure to issues you have with your parents while they are still here. There are millions of people who did not have the opportunity to grant the forgiveness to their parents before they left this earth.

Be honest about your feelings. You should always respect your parents, even when they may not respect you. You have the choice to love them from a distance. Your first responsibility is to God, so honoring your parents does not mean that you allow them to use or abuse you. God is our heavenly father. We can carry our burdens to Him and take comfort in knowing His love for us is unconditional. Do not live with the regret of leaving things unresolved. God can do supernaturally what we are unable to do humanly. He can change hearts and give you the peace you desire!

Self-Reflection: Take a moment to answer the following questions.

- What are the first three things you think of when your mother/grandmother comes to mind?
- What have you blamed on your relationship with your mother?
- How have your feelings towards your mother or grandmother been a crutch or hindrance to you?
- How can you move forward and heal from the past hurt?
- What positive traits did the women in your life pass along to you?

Suggested Scripture(s):

"Train up a child in the way he should go; even when he is old he will not depart from it." Proverbs 22:6 (ESV)

"Behold, children are a heritage from the Lord, the fruit of the womb a reward." Psalm 127:3 (ESV)

"My son, keep your father's commandment, and forsake not your mother's teaching." Proverbs 6:20 (ESV)

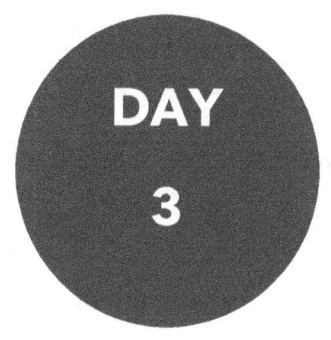

FAMILY TIES

"I am reminded of your sincere faith, a faith that dwelt first in your grandmother Lois and your mother Eunice and now, I am sure, dwells in you as well." 2 Timothy 1:5 (ESV)

We do not choose our families. They have been handpicked for us. Some families are close. Some are distant. Some are just dysfunctional. My grandmother birthed eight sons and two daughters. My mother was the third to the oldest child. I loved my uncles. They were my protectors and the closest thing I had to a father after my parents parted ways when I was five-years-old. I was the only grandchild for the first seven years of my life. Needless to say, I was spoiled rotten by my grandmother, uncles, and aunt. They would buy me great birthday gifts, play board games with me, and comfort me when I was upset. I loved my family.

Southeast Washington, DC was a tough place live in the 80s because of drugs. Drugs were all around us, on every street corner, in our apartment complex, and even outside the carryout. It was hard for people to resist. The economy was bad, and trouble was readily available. I never understood what drugs were or how they could destroy a family until it hit home. When I was twelve-years-old, my mother and her boyfriend had a tumultuous blow-up, so for a few days, I had to stay with one of my uncles and his girlfriend.

My mom brought over my TV and Super Nintendo to keep me preoccupied while I was there. I loved my uncle's girlfriend. She was always nice to me, but I was not comfortable staying, in her Minnesota Avenue apartment. On the first night, I laid on her living room couch tossing and turning unable to fall asleep. Suddenly, I heard the back room door open, and footsteps creak across the apartment hardwood floor. I pretended to be asleep trying hard to keep my eyes shut. The footsteps grew closer and stopped by the couch, so I peeked to see who it was. To my relief, it was just my uncle. I parted my lips to speak, but immediately stopped when I saw him pick up my 19' color TV, and carry it out of the living room. Another set of footsteps hit the hardwood floor; these steps moved with urgency.

It was his girlfriend. "Don't do this!" she said in a pleading whisper.

"I'll be right back," he refuted.

"Your sister is going to kill you if you sell your niece's TV," she warned.

"I'll be back," he repeated as the door to the apartment opened and closed. I laid there with my heart almost beating out of my chest. Where was he going with my TV? I thought. The next day, I learned the harsh reality about one of my favorite uncles. My mother came to the apartment to collect me and my belongings but became angry when she discovered that my television, Super Nintendo, and uncle were nowhere to be found. She slammed the car door. As we drove away, she mumbled, "Damn drug addicts."

Growing up, there have been countless numbers of missing items, broken promises, family disputes, and time apart. Drugs have taken a toll on several family members, and their ability to be who they once were. As I matured, it was easier to acknowledge and see people for who they really are. The key to coping with family members with an addiction of any kind is first to have a clear understanding of what an addiction is.

As much as it hurts us, we have to look at the hold that drugs and alcohol can have on those around us. When something is not an issue for you, it is hard to comprehend the hold it can have on a person. It becomes easy for us to judge, trust me. I was that person. I was bitter, angry and hurt by the things that were taken from me over the years. Each time I thought "This will be the last time."

If you noticed, I said the "things" that were taken from me. As I began to learn more about how addiction controls addicts, I saw that it was not a personal attack. When he stole my belongings, it was not about me. He saw the value in the items, and could not realize the pain his actions caused. It was about the next "fix", not his relationship with me or anyone around him. I grew to learn that things can be replaced. I could not continue to be angry about his actions because he would ultimately be the one who would have to answer for them.

Growing Pains Lesson

Your family will always be your family through all of the fighting and drama. Does this mean you keep giving them permission to hurt you? Absolutely not! You must acknowledge the issue, and work hard not to repeat the pattern. Some of my family thinks I am stuck up, and act like as if I'm too good for them. That is their perception, and I cannot be held in bondage by how others view me. I am at a point in life where I cannot be around negativity and things of the world. If I am uncomfortable in an environment, I remove myself from it. You can respect and love someone, but choose not to be disrespected by them or deal with things that are against your personal morals and values.

Be honest about your feelings, but also take ownership of your actions. You are in control of you. People will only do what you allow. If your parents are financially irresponsible and are constantly draining you of your resources, it is okay to put your foot down. Learn to say "No, I cannot continue to take away from my household to support yours." It is not about being disrespectful or selfish. It's about holding others accountable and not overextending yourself. If someone constantly brings alcohol to your house, and you do not drink it is okay to say "You are welcome here, but leave your liquor at the door."

Mend relationships where possible, and if all options have been exhausted, pray for them, and love them from a distance. If they are meant to be in your life, God can restore the relationship in His timing if we keep ourselves open to the reconciliation. Be empowered to change your family dynamics. Be the light in a potentially dark situation, but most of all do not become a product of your environment.

Self-Reflection: Take a moment to answer the following questions.

- What is your family dynamics?
- Who is the head of your family, and how is your relationship with him or her?

- What are some areas of concerns that you wish to address with your family?

- How would you like to move forward with your family and what part can you play to assist in that happening?

Suggested Scripture(s):

"For the moment all discipline seems painful rather than pleasant, but later it yields the peaceful fruit of righteousness to those who have been trained by it." Hebrews 12:11 (ESV)

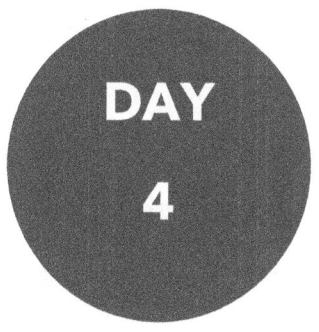

UNTIL WE MEET AGAIN

"Blessed are those who mourn, for they shall be comforted." Matthew 5:4 (ESV)

No two people deal with grief the same. We can never predict how we will respond when we lose a loved one. To achieve peace, we must process our pain. It is not about getting over the loss, but getting through our loss. Celebrate the life of the ones who have passed on. We cannot pray for someone to make it to heaven, but we can find comfort in knowing that God's will, shall be done. When I was seven, my family and I experienced a terrible loss. My grandmother, Virginia Arter, went home to be with the Lord. The news was devastating. Even at the tender age of seven I knew that my life would change drastically from the loss of my grandmother. I remember going to the mall and picking out a navy blue dress with white trim that would be the dress I would wear the day my grandmother was buried.

The day of the funeral our apartment was filled with family members, and as we prepared to exit for the church one of my uncles made the announcement that he felt it would be best for me not to attend the funeral. My mother quickly agreed she told me that I would stay with the neighbor, and she would come back for me. I was extremely upset. I cried and pleaded wanting to say goodbye to my grandmother but, to no avail. I was taken to a neighbor's apartment and waited for my mother to return from the funeral. A couple of hours later my mother returned to pick me up and take me to the repast. Family, friends, and neighbors all crowded the church's community room. Everyone spoke and smiled at me as if I had no idea of what was going on. I resented my family for keeping me from the funeral. I was only seven-years-old, but I understood the magnitude of the loss. I was hurt, upset, and confused. How could they keep me from having closure with my grandmother, I thought. That was a sore spot for me for years to come.

Growing Pains Life Lessons

Grief is a natural response to loss. Attempting to bury grief causes it to manifest in other areas of our lives. When we suppress our grief, we begin to shut-out friends and family, experience depression, lash out in anger, turn to drugs or alcohol, or anything to help us forget about the pain. When dealing with grief, it is important to remain positive. You must fight the urge to give up. Pain sometimes feels unbearable, but it is an important part of our grieving process.

There are different stages of grief:

Shock and Denial

Your initial response to the news of your loved one no longer being with you is shock. The shock comes because we are unable to fathom life without them. The shock we feel when we first experience loss sometimes turns into denial. We say things like "this is not true," or "this can't be real".

Despair and Depression

Some may feel depression and despair. Normal tasks become difficult to focus on. The slightest situation or possession can bring up a memory of the person lost.

Recovery

The goal of grieving is not to eliminate the pain or the memories of our loss. In this stage, one shows a new interest in daily activities and begins to function normally day-to-day. The goal is to reorganize one's life. This requires us to reposition the loss. While the loss is an important part of life, it should not be the center.

When we fail to go through the grief process, unresolved feelings linger. For a long time, I felt my family had been inconsiderate of my feelings by declining me the opportunity to attend my grandmother's funeral. In hindsight, I can see how they were trying to protect me from the pain of losing her. I was a little girl, so they may have thought it was too much for me to experience. Maybe they were right. No one knows how I would have responded if I had physically been there. We will never know. If you were not able to receive closure the way you desired, create your own closure. Pray for healing from your loss. Have a memorial service in honor of your loved one. You can celebrate them in your own way. No one can ever take away the memories and love that you once shared.

Self-Reflection: Take a moment to do the following activity

- Write a letter to someone you have lost. Express your feelings about their absence in your life.

Suggested Scripture(s)

"Blessed are those who mourn, for they will be comforted." Matthew 5:4 (ESV)

"Praise be to the God and Father of our Lord Jesus Christ, the Father of compassion and the God of all comfort, who comforts

us in all our troubles, so that we can comfort those in any trouble with the comfort we ourselves receive from God." 2 Corinthians 1:3-4 (ESV)

"When you pass through the waters, I will be with you; and when you pass through the rivers, they will not sweep over you. When you walk through the fire, you will not be burned; the flames will not set you ablaze." Isaiah 43:2 (ESV)

"God is our refuge and strength, an ever-present help in trouble. Therefore we will not fear, though the earth give way and the mountains fall into the heart of the sea." Psalm 46:1-2 (ESV)

"He will wipe every tear from their eyes. There will be no more death' or mourning or crying or pain, for the old order of things has passed away." Revelation 21:4 (ESV)

COUNT IT ALL JOY

"Consider it pure joy, my brothers, whenever you face trials of many kinds, because you know that the testing of your faith develops perseverance." James 1:2-3 (ESV)

If you are reading this, you made it. Your childhood did not break you. Your bad choices did not hinder you. Toxic relationships have not ruined you. Nothing that hurt you had the power to kill you. You made it! Given your current situation, you may not feel like much of an accomplishment. Just take a moment and think about where you could be vs. where you are. You are still living and breathing. You have been bruised, but life did not break you. For that reason, you should count it all joy!

One Sunday, I attended my church not sure what to expect for the day. The title of Pastor Jenkins' message was "Count it All Joy". He referenced the scripture, James 1:2-4. That scripture alone had me speechless. I had never considered that God was allowing me to go through hardships to strengthen me for even bigger trials he knew I would face.

I know it may not seem realistic to celebrate some of your setbacks, but the great thing about starting over is that you have the opportunity to view the situation with a clear head, and God's help. My mother and father separated when I was only five. At the time, I could not understand why she had left, or why he had not come for us. Over the years, I ran into my father at random places, and he always acted the same. He acted more like a friend of the family than a man who had created me with my mother. Our conversations were always superficial: "How are you doing in school? How is your mom?"

Growing up, I did not acknowledge the fact that his absence affected me. For this reason, I always looked to men for love. I swore that when I had my family and children, it would be nothing like the way I grew up. It was painful to be without my father's love and presence.

It wasn't until I was a teenager that I learned the hard truth about my mother and father's relationship. My father had become addicted to drugs, so my mother kept me away to protect me.

For years, I felt cheated of a picture perfect life. I did not understand the magnitude of what my mother's actions had done. She had protected me from an even greater pain than what I had experienced from his absence. I had seen people struggle with addiction. It ruined their lives. If my mother had stayed with my father, she would have run the risk of raising me in a toxic and dangerous environment.

Growing Pains Life Lessons

Even when you think God is not present in your situation, trust that He has His hands on you. Thankfully today, my father is clean and sober. Although we still do not have a relationship, I count it all joy. Be grateful for each experience. Our circumstances are just a part of the plan God has for us. He wants us to be trusting of his promise and have unwavering faith. When we fall apart at every sign of adversity, we show God and those around us that we do not trust in God's promises. We should lead by example even when it feels impossible, especially when it feel impossible! With every trial, there is a potential for a triumph.

Maybe you are still upset about your parents' divorce. It's okay to acknowledge your hurt, but we must be understanding and seek clarity on the entire situation. Divorcing may have been the best option to ensure your safety, peace of mind, and care. Imagine how damaging it could have been for you and your siblings to keep enduring the things your parents experienced behind closed doors. You may feel the void of not having your parents together, but get to the root of your feelings, and allow yourself to heal. We have to do our part to find the blessing in the things that have hurt us. Meet every trial and tribulation with prayer and supplication.

Self-Reflection: Take a moment to answer the following questions.

- What can you do to look beyond your frustrations when your life does not go as planned?
- Name three difficult circumstances that you are grateful for?
- How can you work to see past the frustration when things don't go as planned?

Suggested Scriptures:

"May the God of hope fill you with all joy and peace in believing, so that by the power of the Holy Spirit you may abound in hope." Romans 15:13 (ESV)

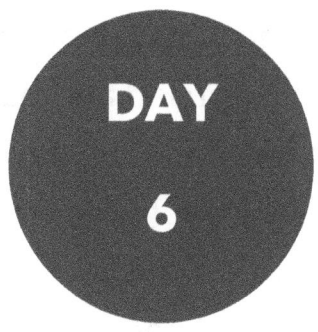

RELEASE GUILT & SHAME

"Therefore, if anyone is in Christ, he is a new creation. The old has passed away; behold, the new has come." 2 Corinthians 5:17 (ESV)

At some point in our lives, we all have had to deal with feeling guilty or ashamed about something we have done, said, or even thought. Sometimes the guilt is self-inflicted, while other times it is perpetuated by outside forces. Unfortunately, some guilt is a little harder to let go than others. I was on a business trip, and I could not have been happier to be away from the hustle and bustle of my day-to-day life. I arrived at my hotel, got settled and decided to eat dinner at a restaurant in the hotel. I was so engrossed in my phone that I hadn't noticed when an old friend from college sat down at my table. I was surprised and happy to see him. What were the chances that he would be staying at the same place as me hundreds of miles from home? I hadn't seen Xavier in years, but he was so easy on the eyes and his charm had not faded. We caught up over dinner, talked about our business ventures and reminisced about the good 'ole days of undergrad. After a couple of hours, the jet lag set in, and I told him I was going to turn in for the night. He asked for my number so that we could connect and possibly go for dinner the next night. I obliged, and we exchanged numbers. The next day I was bombarded with meeting after meeting and was finally back in my room relaxing when I got a text inviting me to dinner. I agreed, and we met in the lobby that evening. After such a draining day I longed for some good conversation. Once again, we laughed and reminisced over dinner.

"So, what are you doing later?" He asked.

"Later when?" I asked looking at my phone. It was already 11 o'clock. "I'm about to go to bed," I responded without giving him a chance to answer my question. We said our goodbye's and I returned to my room, showered, and settled into bed. Suddenly, I got a text from Xavier. Apparently, he wanted to come over and "chill". I stared at the phone for several minutes. There is always an awkward pause before we decide to do the right thing or the wrong thing. I went back and forth in my head about what I should do. On one hand, I wanted to enjoy his company. On the other hand, I knew that it was a slippery slope to hang out with him in my room.

I should have ignored the text and went to bed, but that would have been too much like right. Instead, I texted him my room number and waited for him to arrive. I was naive and thought that I would be able to handle my own, and fight the temptation to do more than chill. In the midst, I was in bliss. He told me how he had thought about me so much over the years, and that I was everything he expected. I felt proud although I shouldn't have. The next day we chatted for a few and said our goodbyes. It was time for us to go our separate ways and return back to our respective lives.

I returned home and tried to clear my mind of what had transpired. I did not want to become sprung. We lived in different areas, and I wondered if we could make the long distance thing work? I went to check my Facebook and saw that Xavier had sent me a friend request and an instant message to if I had made it home safely. I accepted it and responded to his message. He went on to say he had a great time, and wanted to see me again when he came into town. I blushed. I looked forward to seeing him again as well.

After we had finished messaging, I decided to check out his page. After all, we hadn't seen each other in four years. I wanted to know what he had been doing. As soon as I began to scroll down the page, I was stopped dead in my tracks. Relationship status: Married. I felt a lump in my throat. I thought I was going to be sick. Married? How? When? I was devastated. Did he have a ring on? I was prone to always checking a man's hand before I even looked twice at him. How could I have missed it? How could he not tell me?

It was bad enough that I had fornicated, but now I had become the other woman without even knowing it! I was young and not well versed in affairs, so I did not know what to do. Should I flip out on him? Should I tell her? I sought counsel from a friend who convinced me to leave it alone without saying or doing anything. So, I did just that. I unfriended him and tried to forget it ever happened, but my gut wouldn't let me. I repented to God and prayed for forgiveness. Although I believed that God had forgiven me, I couldn't forgive myself. I had created soul ties that were never meant to be.

I carried that burden around for years. It was not until I had joined the Queen Esther Ministry at my church that I began to be honest with myself, and work through my anger and embarrassment. I had to do the work required to learn to let go of my guilt and shame. The only way I could be free and at peace was by forgiving myself for the decisions I had made.

Growing Pains Life Lessons

The deeper we try to bury the things we are ashamed of the more they control us. When we are open and honest with ourselves, we never feel indebted to someone else, even if that someone is us. We are our own worst critics. We cannot heal unless we get out of our own heads. I learned that allowing my embarrassment to hold me hostage kept me in bondage. Once I forgave myself and made amends with my actions, I was able to move forward. The enemy could no longer hold it over my head.

Although the Bible says that all sin carries the same weight, we have a tendency to rank sin based on our personal feelings. Killing someone was not the same as fornication, and lying was nowhere as bad as stealing, right? Wrong! That was my problem. I believed in the sanctity of marriage and in my mind I had committed the ultimate sin. God allowed me to see what the truth was. When it came down to it, I realized God's love was sufficient. Jesus Christ had died for my sins. By his blood, I was saved and my multitude of sins was covered.

Self-Reflection: Take a moment to complete the following questions.

- Are you still beating yourself up over something you have done wrong? If so, why?

- Have you addressed the issue with yourself, God, and the others involved?

Pray to God for peace and meditate on the scriptures below:

Suggested Scripture(s):

"If we confess our sins, he is faithful and just to forgive us our sins and to cleanse us from all unrighteousness." 1 John 1:9 (ESV)

"Just so, I tell you, there will be more joy in heaven over one sinner who repents than over ninety-nine righteous persons who need no repentance." Luke 15:7 (ESV)

PRAY WITHOUT CEASING

When you are tempted, hold the temptation before God and ask for His help. When you experience something good and beautiful, immediately thank the Lord for it. When you see evil around you, you ask God to make it right and to use you toward that end, if that is His will.

"For God is my witness, whom I serve with my spirit in the gospel of His Son that without ceasing I make mentions of you always in my prayers."
Romans 1:9 (ESV)

We have to prepare for what we ask for. If you are praying for a new job, you also need to be preparing for it. Once during a sermon, I recall a pastor saying, "You're waiting on God, but God is waiting on you!" That truth made me shout. I knew God was talking to me.

Before that moment, if someone had asked me if I was preparing for what I had been praying for, I would have quickly said yes. However, in all actuality, I could have been doing more, and finishing what I started.

I wanted God to move onto the next thing while I was still in the midst of working on the first thing. If I can be transparent with you, I had a habit of moving on from one thing to another, one hobby to another, and sometimes one man to another. I got bored with it, it became too much work and/or I realized the end wouldn't justify the means. While it's great to be able to put down things that don't serve your purpose, if you're putting down everything you pick up, you may want to stop and evaluate your selection process.

If you're relocating or switching gears in your career every other year, you don't have a chance to grow roots and set a steady foundation for yourself. You can't get what you've been praying for, because you're unprepared. God will give us the tools, the desires and the instruction, but we have to have the will to put it into application. Have you ever heard the saying that practice makes perfect? Well, that is not always true. Make time for God, and God will make time for you. He wants our time and attention. We cannot just give it to Him when we're in need or when things are rough. We have to be consistent and intentional.

Think about athletes and how much they train and run plays. On game day, they go against other athletes who have also trained. So that day is not about being perfect because there's no guarantee. You can depend on the permanence of what you learned and know that your preparation will allow you to switch your strategy and be prepared for whatever may come your way. That is what God desires for us to do. He wants us first to pray and find out if our desires are his desires.

Have we thought them through from beginning to end before we go before God and ask? He wants us to come to Him with a prepared posture. He needs to know that if He gives us the very things we are praying for we will be ready to receive and walk in our purpose. God rewards the diligent. There is power in bible study. Make time for corporate prayer and fellowship. I honestly did not go frequently. I always said I was too busy. I didn't make it a priority. The one thing I did consistently was being inconsistent. I prayed about things at the moment and then moved on.

Now just like everything else, I schedule the time, I block it out and commit to making it happen. God loves our obedience. When I was a babe in Christ, I expected what God fed me on Sunday to be sufficient for the entire week. I now know that I have to have daily alone time with God in order to withstand whatever issues come my way. He has the power to give us unspeakable peace if we seek him for it.

Think about it like this. Imagine that your family has a feast. The spread is almost a mile long with all your favorite foods and desserts to top it off. You eat until your heart is content. You're full and satisfied for the rest of the day. The next day rolls around, and you get a little grumble in your stomach. Even though you had the large meal yesterday, you're hungry again. So, you eat a little something to satisfy you. Well the next day, you wake up and now you are starving. That Sunday Dinner is now a distant memory and you're looking for something else to fulfill you. It works the same way with our fellowship and meditation on God's Word. Sunday is simply not enough.

Growing Pains Life Lessons

The same way your body craves food is the same way your spirit craves the word of God. It needs something daily to sustain you. Sunday just isn't enough. Think of all the people we have to encounter in a week, issues that arise, frustrations that surface and things big and small that can easily take us out of our peacefulness. That's why we need to obtain pure joy. We need to feed ourselves and build up our armor of God so that we can withstand whatever trials come our way.

Self-Reflection: Take a moment to answer the following questions.

- What does your prayer life look like?

- What area of your life are you seeking a movement from God (i.e. career, finances, love)?

- What can you do to improve your prayer/ quiet time with God?

Suggested Scripture(s):

"And he told them a parable to the effect that they ought always to pray and not lose heart." Luke 18:1 (ESV)

"Pray then like this: "Our Father in heaven, hallowed be your name. Your kingdom come, your will be done, on earth as it is in heaven. Give us this day our daily bread, and forgive us our debts, as we also have forgiven our debtors. And lead us not into temptation, but deliver us from evil." Matthew 6:9-13 (ESV)

EMOTIONAL ROLLERCOASTER

"A fool gives full vent to his spirit, but a wise man quietly holds it back" Proverbs 29:11 (ESV)

I am an emotional woman. There, I admit it! I found myself often being led by my heart before I let my head get involved. I loved hard, cared deeply, and was hurt easily. My emotions dictated much of how I lived my life. Have you ever been on a rollercoaster? Against my better judgment, I have been swayed into riding several over the years. Always with the promise that "it will be fun!" For some reason, I always believed them. I would climb up to the top of an overwhelming staircase and look down even though I am afraid of heights. I would allow them to strap me into the ride, and take me on a ride they assured me would be "fun." In the beginning, the anticipation was thrilling. I always thought to myself, maybe it'll be enjoyable this time. Then, the dips in the tracks would come, and the constant jerks caused my stomach to get in knots. Then, there's the final plunge at the end that made me feel as though I was going to lose my breakfast, lunch, and dinner.

Finally, we would come to a screeching halt, and I would feel awful. Once again, I would be upset that I allowed someone to talk me into a situation I did not want to be in only for it to end how I already knew it would. I don't like rollercoasters, but I continuously found myself where I did not want to be. Bottling up our emotions, whether good or bad, is unhealthy and can cause us to be off balance.

In undergrad, all the freshmen were automatically on the utility crew when we did banquets and events for our major. We had to do most of the grunt work like pulling trash, sweeping and mopping the floors, and washing dishes. One time, my friend Pam and I were working on utility during dinner theater. We were so consumed with getting all the dishes cleaned for the dish room, we hadn't realized that all the other students had disappeared from the hall.

We went to find everyone and realized people were eating in the Bailey Thomas room.

"Why didn't anyone tell me that we were going on break?" I asked a nearby friend.

"I don't know," he responded and shrugged it off. Pam and I went to wash our hands and grab some food. When we arrived at the platters, we saw that they were all empty. We asked one of the student managers when the rest of the food would come out. To our surprise, he said that there was no more food, and they weren't making any more.

I could not believe my ears. We had been working on our feet for four hours without a break. Now we weren't going to be able to eat until the event was over. I quickly became angry and proceeded to go off on him.

"This doesn't make any sense," I snapped. "You're supposed to be the manager. You should have made sure that we had something to eat." I yelled. The room got quiet, and everyone's attention went to me. I was in such a rage, I didn't pay attention to the stares from my peers. I continued to yell at the manager until I felt vindicated.

I stormed out and went into the hall. Pam followed behind me laughing all the way, "I can't believe you went off like that," she said. A few minutes later, another student manager came out and said that they were making us a pizza and that it would be ready in a few minutes. I felt vindicated when I returned to the room. People were laughing and joking about how I had embarrassed our classmate. As my anger subsided, I started to feel a pang of remorse. I could have stayed calm even though he was rude. It was unnecessary for me to act worst than he did. I had let my emotions get the best of me.

Growing Pains Life Lessons

Our emotions control how we function. When we act out of emotion, we say and do things we later regret. You may be able to apologize or even buy a present, but once things are said, they can damage relationships, as well as yourself. How many friendships have you lost, family members have you been estranged from, or relationships have ended based on your emotions? We need to show restraint and gain control over our mind and our emotions. It is important for us to stop, process, and think before we speak in high pressured situations. It may be hard to gain control of yourself; however, it may be even harder to gain back trust and change people's perception of you when you allow your emotions to get the best of you.

Self-Reflection: Take moment to answer the following questions.

- How do you keep your emotions in tact?
- How can you adjust the way you display your emotions?

- What outlet do you have to express yourself when you are upset?

Suggested Scripture(s)

"And let steadfastness have its full effect, that you may be perfect and complete, lacking in nothing." James 1:4 (ESV)

"For whatever was written in former days was written for our instruction, that through endurance and through the encouragement of the Scriptures we might have hope." Romans 15:4 (ESV)

DAY 9

HOW DO YOU ENDURE?

"More than that, we rejoice in our sufferings, knowing that suffering produces endurance, and endurance produces character, and character produces hope" Romans 5:3-4 (ESV)

Have you ever been to the doctor and they put the Velcro cuff on you to take your blood pressure? At first, it doesn't bother you. You barely notice that the cuff is applying pressure. As they begin to squeeze, the cuff begins to get tighter and tighter around your arm. You can't move. Any movement will disrupt the reading. Sometimes, it gets so tight that you're ready to scream or pass out. Before you can even mumble a sound, it's over. Your reading pops up, and they remove the cuff. You feel silly for even wincing at the short time you had to feel uncomfortable for you to get something you really needed.

That's what we need to think of when we think of endurance. Sometimes there is no get-out-of-jail-free card we can use when we're up against life's obstacles. We go through seasons where everything seems to be going wrong. Although we do our best and try to stay positive, the weight of the world can surely become too heavy for us to bear. Even in times of dismay, it's important for us to push through in the face of adversity. Every test will lead to a testimony. Sometimes we don't realize how strong we are until we have to endure something we never thought we would make it through.

I took a four-year break in between my undergrad and grad program. I worked full-time and had an active social life. Also, I did my part in the community. In all of this, there was still a void. I wanted more education. I prayed that getting a master's degree would lead to more opportunities, so I signed up for an accelerated graduate degree program. Being out of school for over four years made it hard to get back into the swing of things. Taking an 8-week course that would have normally been 16 weeks quickly showed me that I would need to change my way of thinking to make it through this program. I worked daily from 9 am to 5 pm and then rushed to my classes from 5 pm to 10 pm.

I got very little sleep and even less time to socialize. I quickly became accustomed to surviving off 5 Hour Energy drinks. I was trying to juggle it all. My job was very demanding. My cohorts were parents, full-time employees, husbands, and wives. There was no room for excuses. We all were dealing with daily struggles, but had to meet the deadlines if we ever expected to complete the program. There were some times where I doubted myself and thought I had made a mistake. Was it worth it to kill myself to get another degree? One part of me struggled and swore up and down that it was just a piece of paper. Deep down inside I knew that I needed it to move on and obtain a different career.

After each completed course, I felt a little more at ease with my decision to stick it out. Despair returned during my final semester when I realized I would have to take a comprehensive exam of everything I had learned up until that point. "How am I even supposed to study for something like this?" I asked myself. I had a 4.0 GPA, and I was confident that I would pass my last four courses, but were they seriously telling me I needed to pass another exam to graduate?

Needless to say, I studied and prayed like I never had before. Six weeks after the exam, I finally received my letter confirming I had passed and was on target to graduate. Two years felt like an eternity until it was all over. The gratification I felt earning that degree in spite of my hectic experience was such a priceless feeling. The late nights, group projects, and 15 and 20 Page papers quickly became a distant memory. It felt like such a small feat for what I achieved.

Life is a marathon, not a sprint I don't know about you, but I just knew that my 30s would be better than my 20s. I was excited about the promise of what was in store. I had my vision board prepared, and my mind focused on God. I was floating on air until my bubble burst. I started to experience one frustration after another. I experience drama on my job, health issues, and failing relationships with friends and my significant other. Things became overwhelming. I was weak and weary. I went home after work one night, and I was completely drained. I passed out for an hour and woke up with a terrible headache. I got up and decided to take myself out to dinner, and have a date night with God. I drove to one of my favorite restaurants. While I waited, I prayed and then opened up my "Marriage A to Z workbook for Singles" to do some studying. I realized I was on the letter E, and the lesson was about endurance.

It posed a question that I had not considered. What does it mean to endure? I quickly wrote, "enduring means to withstand in times of difficulty or hardships." Then I added, "without complaining." Before the ink could dry on the page, I felt convicted. I felt an immediate tug and heard God's voice saying, "Well if you know what to do and how you should do it, why aren't you doing it?" I smiled to myself and relief washed over me. Thank you, Jesus, I said softly aloud to myself. I spent the rest of my dinner eating, reading the workbook, and listening to God's word.

When I got into the car, I began to pray and worship God even more. I cried out to Him and thanked Him for being so wonderful. He gave me comfort and reassurance.

Growing Pains Life Lessons

God is always available to us if we seek him. He can speak to us through so many avenues. He is constantly strengthening us. He knows that we have the capacity to handle it when we rely on His abilities and not our own. If we can endure the task, our reward will be greater than what we could have ever asked or imagined. During our despair, it feels impossible. It's daunting and sometimes feels unrealistic, but in the end, we walk away filling reassured, satisfied, fulfilled, and stronger than when we started. That's the power of endurance.

Self-Reflection: Take a moment to answer the following questions.

- What does enduring mean to you?
- What is an area in your life that God is asking you to endure?
- How do you cope with trials?

Suggested Scripture(s):

"More than that, we rejoice in our sufferings, knowing that suffering produces endurance, and endurance produces character, and character produces hope," Romans 5:3-4 (ESV)

DAY 10

NEGATIVE NANCY

"Let no corrupting talk come out of your mouths, but only such as is good for building up, as fits the occasion, that it may give grace to those who hear." Ephesians 4:29 (ESV)

Do you get annoyed when Pharell's song "Because I'm Happy" comes on? If so, you may not be in a good head space. Why do chipper people annoy us? What can make him that happy that he felt the need to sing about it? Maybe he's doing what we all need to do. Choosing to be happy! Believe it or not, happiness is a choice. It is not to say that things will not fall apart around you, but it means that you will choose to maintain in spite of what is happening around you. I know you may feel that it is easier said than done.

Colossians 3:2 tells us "Set your minds on things above, not on earthly things." We have to choose to be happy. Don't live in negativity.

Do not allow your pain to overshadow someone else's joy. It is one thing to say things in love; it is another to be malicious. Sometimes when we are not happy with our situations, it is hard for us to celebrate others. I love my Pastor who always reminds us that if God is blessing others, be excited because it means that He is in your neighborhood. How can you not get excited about that?

We cannot harbor negative thoughts and feelings toward others and expect God to continue to bless us. If you think you are never going to get the promotion at your job, then you are putting those thoughts into the atmosphere, which changes your mindset and your actions. Instead of continuing to do a great job you start slacking off, and acting careless, and as you predicted you do not get your promotion.

It wasn't because you were not good enough. You didn't get the promotion because you had already come to a resolve in your mind, so your attitude towards your performance shifted. When we think positively, our mind sends signals to our body to respond positively. When we think with a positive mindset, everything always works for our good, even when it doesn't work in our favor.

Growing Pains Life Lessons

You have to believe it before you see it. You can't have negative thoughts and lead a positive life. Capture each negative thought and cancel it out of your mind. The enemy can hear your thoughts just like God can. He knows your weaknesses. You control the doorway to your mind. God can expedite your situation. The battle is in our minds. Give yourself permission to overcome and obtain your dreams.

You cannot allow outside elements to decide if you are going to be happy or not. Your joy cannot be contingent upon the weather, the traffic on your daily commute or even a good morning text from a crush. Happiness is a choice, and we have to make that choice every day. It took me some time to come to the realization that I was not genuinely happy. I was happy based on what was going on around me. I would start my day pumped up feeling like a million bucks. As soon as things got crazy in a staff meeting or I received a text about canceled plans, I became a sour puss. I was tired of being on an emotional roller coaster. The irony was that I was the one standing at the controls.

It is a continuous effort to be a positive person. A bad day does not mean that you are going to have a bad week. Instead of feeling depressed about ending your weekends and going back to work on Monday, be grateful that you have a job. We often rush through the week just to get to Friday again to feel a momentary joy, not realizing that during the rest of the week, life is passing us. If you are that miserable, change your lifestyle, your job, your home life, and above else change your mindset. If you are the only bright spot on your job, be that for yourself. You are only as happy as you choose to be. Happiness is a lifestyle, not a destination.

Self-Reflection: Take a moment to answer the following questions.

- How has your negativity affected your friends, family or significant other?
- What would you do if you could get out of your way?
- How will you deal with negative thoughts moving forward?
- What will be your daily mantra to start and continue on a positive track?

Suggested Scripture(s):

"Whatever is in your heart determines what you say." Matthew 12:34 (ESV)

LOWERED EXPECTATIONS

"And he fixed his attention on them, expecting to receive something from them." Acts 3:5 (ESV)

I once heard a sermon on love and marriage by Pastor Keith Battle. He gave the example of a woman's 25th birthday, and how she knows her husband is taking her out for a birthday dinner. She thinks to herself, "It would be so romantic if he gives me 25 long stem red roses since I'm turning 25." She gets to the restaurant, and her husband presents her with 12 long stem red roses. The husband thinks he did a good job, but the wife is not fully satisfied. The roses could be gorgeous, but because she already set the expectancy in her mind that she desired 25 roses, the 12 will not be enough.

I hate to be the bearer of bad news, but I have to tell you there's a chance that you will be disappointed expecting someone to say what you want to hear, or respond to things the way you would. It is important that we learn the difference between standards and expectations. It is okay to tell or show people how to treat you, to stand up for yourself and decide not to accept a certain behavior, or even voice your wants and needs.

Now what we should not do is have the expectation that people will go above and beyond for us because that is what we would do for them. We should not have an expectation for people to read our minds either. I know it's a shocking blow. Trust me, I felt the same way when I came to the painful realization time, and time, and time again. I also realized that if I did not change my way of thinking, I would constantly be disappointed.

Prime example, one of my dear friends. He's very outgoing, friendly and outspoken. He sometimes desires to be the center of attention. I always have to get him to mellow out, and let him know when he's doing too much. Well, one day he came to me and told me he was going to order a customized cake for one of our mutual friends' birthday. I told him that was cool and asked him how much the cake would be. He said he knew the person who was going to do it, so it was only going to cost him $80.00. I almost choked at the announcement. My friends were both still college students. Although every birthday is important, he was only turning 23, so this was not a milestone birthday. I tried not to be a party pooper but suggested that he got our friend, a smaller cake and another gift that he would be able to have as a keepsake.

I told him that he could get a cake with a picture on it from BJs for a fraction of the price, and still have money left over to do something else for him if he wanted to. Well, he agreed, and scratched the idea of getting the custom cake. Two days, later he stopped by to inform me that he went ahead and ordered the $80.00 customized cake. All I could do was shake my head. "Okay, but I'm telling you I think it's too much" I warned. Unfortunately, my wise counsel fell on deaf ears.

That weekend, my friends had the birthday dinner where the cake would be presented. I had another engagement, so I did not make it. Monday I texted my friend to ask how everything went. I found out that my friend didn't receive the response he thought he should have for such an expensive cake. You see, the birthday boy had just been surprised with a cake at work. By the time he made it to the dinner party, he was all caked out. To add insult to injury he and his friends were too full from dinner to eat the cake. They ate a small part of the cake and began to give it to the restaurant employees and other random guests to get rid of it. To put it very lightly, my dear friend was angry, and he felt unappreciated. In fact, he brought it up continuously for several months. Finally, I got tired of hearing about the cake fiasco and decided to intervene. I explained to him that when we build up our expectations of how something is going to go, we leave ourselves vulnerable to disappointment.

Growing Pains Life Lessons

Nothing is 100% absolute! We should do things for others because we want to, without desiring anything in return. It is okay to voice concern if a friend doesn't seem appreciative. Keep in mind that people do not always do as we desire them to. I told him that in the future, we should do things for others and have no expectations of them to do something or respond in return. He said that he understood and would not make the same mistake again.

We need to be grateful, do things out of the goodness of our hearts and have no expectations in return. Make the necessary adjustments to reduce your frustrations by having no expectations and taking each moment as it comes.

Self-Reflection: Take a moment to complete the following questions:

- Can you think of a time where you expected something to go a certain way, and it did not?

- List three ways you can manage your expectations of others?

- Are you giving more to others with the expectations or something in return? Why or why not?

Suggested Scripture(s):

"Know that wisdom is such to your soul; if you find it, there will be a future, and your hope will not be cut off." Proverbs 24:14 (ESV)

PEOPLE PLEASERS

"And he who sent me is with me. He has not left me alone, for I always do the things that are pleasing to him." John 8:29 (ESV)

I know some of you are saying, what's wrong with wanting to please others? You are supposed to be giving and supportive to others. Very true. There is nothing wrong with helping a friend move, babysitting for a relative or even giving a friend a lift to the airport, but when does it become too much? How much is your generosity really costing you? It is not always about money. Sometimes it's about time. Your time is valuable. You can always earn more money, but time is priceless and something you will never be able to regain.

Being a people pleaser stems from a need to feel valued or important. We desire to make others happy in hopes that someone will notice our efforts and praise us accordingly. This usually begins to manifest itself in our childhood. We recognize that our parents celebrate us when we make good grades, or score the winning shot at our basketball game, so to continue to gain that display of emotion, we continue to do things to get their attention.

Think of your child, younger sibling, or even yourself as a child. When you built something cool with your leggos or drew a family portrait, you wanted to run and show your parents. You wanted them to share in your excitement. If they didn't, you may have jumped up and down, or kept trying to shove it in their face to get their attention. That is where the need to please others was born.

This can be a dangerous problem to have. Sacrificing yourself for the benefit of others can lead you down a road of becoming a "yes man". I quickly developed that title within my group of friends. I was always going above and beyond to please others because I liked feeling appreciated. I mean, what sane person wants to drive 45 minutes one way to pick someone up, drive them another hour to work and then 30 minutes back home? No one! Unfortunately, I did it. This is not about being a good person because I think that people would consider me to be a great person.

The problem lied within my motives. Sometimes, I did for others because I wanted to feel important. Sometimes, I did it just because I was afraid to say no in fear of them being mad. Seldom did I do it because I wanted to. Now, it is great to do for others, and be selfless. However, when we do things to get praise or approval from man, God is not pleased.

Growing Pains Life Lessons

Our goal should not be to do what is pleasing to man, but what God calls us to do and what is pleasing in His sight. "For am I now seeking the approval of man, or of God? Or am I trying to please man? If I were still trying to please man, I would not be a servant of Christ." Galatians 1:10 (ESV)

We need to do a self-check and look at what is driving us to please others. Is it worth giving what we have to sacrifice, to gain the approval of others? It is important to do things for the right reasons and with pure intentions. Do not overextend yourself to appease people. Help and do what you can within your means, but be sure that what you do for others is not causing damage to you.

Self-Reflection: Take a moment to answer the following questions:

- Are you or someone you know a people pleaser? If so, where did the need to be a people pleaser stem from?

- What do you think will happen if you stop seeking to please others?

- Are you giving more to others than you are giving to yourself, if so why?

- How can you balance sacrificing yourself for others?

Suggested Scripture(s):

"Just as I try to please everyone in everything I do, not seeking my own advantage, but that of many, that they may be saved." 1 Corinthians 10:33 (ESV)

MY BEST FRIEND

By: Stephanie L. Randall

When I think of my best friend

It should be someone who was supportive from the beginning

and will stay to the end.

My best friend will encourage me to go to church,

a true friend who won't judge me based on the brand of my shirt.

I want a best friend who is willing to be a guide for me,

and no matter how difficult the conversation,

I know that they will never lie to me.

See when someone is truly your best friend

they are there when you call,

and whatever your burdens are

they are willing to accept them all.

My best friend knows the word

and put scriptures in my heart

and even when they're not around

I still know we're never far apart.

And, God, when I really thought things through,

I clearly saw my true best friend is you.

WHAT ABOUT YOUR FRIENDS?

"A man of many companions may come to ruin, but there is a friend who sticks closer than a brother." Proverbs 18:24 (ESV)

How many friends do you have? No, I don't mean your coworkers who you see you Monday through Friday. I don't mean your nail tech or your hairdresser. I mean real, true, blue friends; friends who will pray for you, and stand by your side as you weather the storm. We all have associates we call for particular things like to talk about our favorite TV shows, complain about our day, or ask for restaurant suggestions. How many friends do you have? The people you surround yourself with can make or break you. If you are surrounding yourself with positive, supportive, and loving people who have your best interests at heart, you can be at ease and reduce the probability of frienemies within your circle.

When we allow people into our live who do not share our same character, values, or morals, we make ourselves susceptible to drama and frustration. *"Whoever walks with the wise becomes wise, but the companion of fools will suffer harm." Proverbs 13:20 (ESV)*

If I were to be honest, I once called everyone my friend. I used the word loosely without understanding that it should have been earned and not just given. Some believed I was too naive "you're too friendly," they would say. I prided myself on being a people person. I liked being able to meet new people, make news friends, and create bonds wherever I went.

I learned a real lesson about friendship. This lesson came at the age of 23. For years, I was so angry at a female I once thought was my friend. Leah and I had gone to undergrad together and even had the same major. We hung in the same circles, and I considered her a friend. I was a year ahead of her, so when she graduated, I helped out at her party. Now we were far from best friends, but she was, however, best friends with my roommate, Kera so she came by the house occasionally. We had another roommate named Chauncey, a guy I had previously dated. I had been in love with him since I was 16 years old. We had been on and off over the years, but I was hoping we would one day get it together. One night, Leah and I hung out, and she ended up staying over. We stayed up late and talked about my history with Chauncey and how crazy relationships were in general. I still had feelings for Chauncey, but he was not ready to be in a serious relationship, so we dated other people.

The next morning Kera, Leah, and I were in the kitchen when Chauncey walked in. He said his good mornings, grabbed his breakfast and went back downstairs to his bedroom. When he left, Leah commented about how fine he was. I reminded her of the story I had previously told her about Chauncey and I dating. She said she thought he was attractive. I agreed but told her that he was definitely off limits. She shrugged it off and we continued with breakfast.

One night Kera and Leah went out, but when they returned to the house, Leah said her truck was overheating. She asked me if I could wake Chauncey and ask him to take a look at it. I was hesitant because he had to get up early for work, and got cranky when his sleep was disturbed. After much pleading, I reluctantly gave in and called to ask him to come outside to take a look at the truck. He went outside with Kera to look at the truck. I hung out in the living room to finish watching my show that was on TV.

About 30 minutes had passed before Leah and Chauncey came back into the house. Kera had already gone to bed, and I was heading to bed as well. Leah asked what we were about to do. I told her it was 11 o'clock on a weeknight, so we were about to go to bed. There was an awkward pause, so I wished her a goodnight. She said goodbye and headed home. After Leah had left Chauncey looked at me and laughed. "You are such a blocker," he said. I was caught off guard by his statement.

"What am I trying to block? Are you interested in her?" I asked. He shook his head but did not say anything. "Why would you want to sleep with someone who I'm cool with?" I asked disgusted at the thought of him and Leah together.

"Who said I did?" He asked as he walked downstairs.

A few weeks later, Leah returned to the house I assumed to see Kera. To my surprise, she went downstairs to hang out with Chauncey. I was upset and confused about what was going on. After they had been downstairs for over an hour, I almost lost my mind. I have to be honest. I was saved, but trust me, that night I was in my flesh! Lol. I grabbed my cellphone and headed outside. I paced our quiet, tree-lined street, as I called one of my best friends, Jarra, to tell her what was transpiring. She talked to me for what felt like an eternity trying to calm me down, and keep me from confronting the Leah, whom I thought was my friend, and Chauncey, whom I thought cared enough not to hook up with my friends.

I eventually went back in the house and cried myself to sleep. I felt betrayed. Their tryst was short-lived, but the damage lingered. I was hurt and angry with both of them, then more with Leah in the end. I had poured out my feelings to her, told her how I felt about him, and she had still pursued him. She could not understand her error. Chauncey told me that she did not consider us friends, but just "associates." The news hit me like a ton of bricks. From that point on I not only stopped thinking of her as a friend, but I considered her an enemy. This made it extremely difficult given we had several friends in common. That did not stop me from getting nauseous when I saw her, getting angry when I heard her speak, or rolling my eyes at the sound of her name being mentioned.

Pretty soon, I had to take the blame off of her and place it on me. I was holding her to a code she had no interest in being a part of. I had expected her to follow the unwritten rules. Although I told her how I felt about this man, she had no regard because she did not value me. Have you heard the saying, be careful who you let in your home because things will start coming up missing like your happiness? That is where I had made the mistake. I let her in and shared my private and intimate thoughts with her with the preconceived idea that we were friends.

Someone once said to me that you want to be around people who celebrate you, not just tolerate you? You do not want to be the pal that people call up when no one else is available. If you have to worry about what people are saying about you when you are not around, then that person should not have the privilege of calling you their friend. Leah had not proven that she could be trusted. Our time and interactions were very superficial, and I had not given our relationship time to mature. She had been friends with Kera for years but did not seem genuine to her either in her times of need. That should have been an inclination of how she would treat me.

Growing Pains Life Lessons

It was still difficult to overcome the hurt or even trust her again for many years. I prayed constantly and talked through my feelings to get to a good place. I had to reflect and realize that they did me a favor. I stopped being hung up on Chauncey, and I learned to give the friendship title sparingly. Our relationship was never the same. After several years, I was able to stop considering her an enemy; not for her, but for me.

Chauncey and I made amends and ended up being great friends. We have been able to be there for each other over the years and are still close friends today. Although Leah never took ownership for what had transpired, I learned that sometimes we have to accept the apology that we may never receive. I have forgiven both of them and moved on.

Self-Reflection: Take a moment to answer the following questions.

- How many frienemies are clinging to your life, and how are you going to get free?

- What attributes do you feel make up a genuine friend, and why?

- What boundaries do you need to incorporate into your friendships?

Suggested Scripture(s):

A friend loves at all times, and a brother is born for adversity." Proverbs 17:17 (ESV)

Do not be deceived: "Bad company corrupts good morals." 1 Corin. 15:33 (ESV)

ANGER & ANIMOSITY

"In your anger do not sin, Do not let the sun go down while you are still angry, and do not give the devil a foothold." Ephesians 4:26 (ESV)

Growing up, I truly enjoyed spending time with my Uncle David. One day when we were riding, I complained to him about someone making me mad. Before I could finish with my rant, he stopped me. "Stephanie, no one can make you do anything. You are in control of your actions and feelings, so you are actually choosing to feel that way. Stop allowing people to control your emotions." I was fourteen, so I was too young to take heed to his advice. Now that I am an adult, it makes complete sense.

We hold grudges against people and stay mad for weeks, months, and even years. We go out of our way to ignore them, do spiteful things or taint their name. The amusing part is that majority of the time, they are not even thinking of us. They sleep peacefully at night while we toss and turn in turmoil. If you constantly say, "I will never forgive them," your heart will believe you and harden towards them. While we think we are punishing others, we are punishing ourselves. I held a grudge against a friend for over eight years. During that period, I would get so irritated seeing her in passing. It took a lot of energy and work to stay mad. Each time I saw her, I would replay the story in my mind over and over again.

After I had graduated from high school, I began working full-time as a receptionist for a local real estate company. I moved back in with my mother to prepare for my own place. One day while I was out and about I ran into Jasmine, a girl that I was tight with in high school. We had lost contact after high school, and were excited to reconnect. We began talking on the phone every day, and hanging out like we had never been apart. I had always felt for Jasmine because she did not have a strong support system. She had lost both of her parents at a young age.

While we were hanging out one day, I asked Jasmine where she lived. To my surprise, she said that she was living with a friend and her family, and paying $300 a month to rent a bedroom. I thought it seemed unfair and kind of pricey. I suggested that we be roommates, since we got along well, and would not have to pay much more for a place of our own. She agreed, and we began preparing to move. We found an apartment and moved in the next year. My mother was really helpful and supportive. She assisted me by giving us a couch, an entertainment center, and a bed for Jasmine. I bought dishes, a new dining room table, and other odds and ends to make our new home complete.

We had a great time staying up late every night talking and catching up; we were inseparable. We both worked two jobs to keep the bills paid. After the necessities, we had money to get our nails done, and hang out on the weekends. Things were going great. One morning while I was getting ready for work, I caught Jasmine doing the unexpected. I walked into my bedroom and saw her going through my purse. I was caught off guard, and clearly so was she. She looked like a deer caught in the headlights. I asked her what she was doing, and she quickly replied, "I thought I left my ID in the purse." The purse was, in fact, hers. She had loaned it to me a few weeks prior, so I halfway understood. We did share things but, I was still uneasy at the sight of her rifling through my belongings.

I shook the uneasy feeling and chalked it up to a mistake. A few months later, I regretted that decision. I arrived home from work to a surprise notice…. An eviction notice! I was speechless. There had to be some mistake, I thought. I paid my rent on time every month. I was confused and angry. I tore the notice off the door and entered the apartment. I called out to Jasmine to see if she was there. She did not answer, so I knocked on her room door. I opened the door and looked in. She had not made it home yet. Before I could close the door back, I caught a glimpse of a piece of mail from Upper Marlboro. Something told me to take a closer look.

When I looked at the letter, I saw that it was addressed to Jasmine and I. It was unopened, so I ripped it open to see what it was. It was from the courthouse, a notice of delinquency for our rent. The notice said we owed a little of $1400.00! I was fuming. I looked down at the table and noticed three other similar envelopes; not one of them had been opened. I took all the notices and headed to the living room. I was beyond angry. How could she have hidden this from me? Our rent was only $730.00 a month, which meant she had not paid her portion of the rent for the last four months. She kept her hair and nails done. She bought new clothes and ate out frequently, but was not paying her rent!

I tried to address her to find out what was going on, but she avoided the subject at all costs. By the grace of God, my mother paid the back rent so we would not get evicted. Things eventually calmed down. After giving her the silent treatment for a few months, I forgave her. Our reconciliation did not last for long. My portion of the rent money suddenly disappeared from my bedroom a few months later. That was my breaking point. I packed my clothes, television, and stereo, and left the rest of my belongings, the apartment and Jasmine behind. I could not live in an environment where I could not trust the person who slept in the room next to me every night. I incurred debt for breaking my lease early but was willing to do what I needed to get out of the situation with Jasmine. When mutual friends asked what happened, I openly divulged every gory detail of my encounter with the roommate from hell. I was so angry and bitter. I disobeyed God for months and held onto my animosity towards Jasmine until God began to deal with me about my actions. How could I call myself a Christian, but constantly speak negatively about the situation? "Do not let any unwholesome talk come out of your mouths, but only what is helpful for building others up according to their needs, that it may benefit those who listen." Ephesians 4:29. I thought about God requiring us to forgive others, as he has forgiven us. Pastor Jenkins had preached about it over and over again. Holding a grudge against her did not serve a purpose. Does this sound familiar?

Growing Pains Life Lessons

When we are hurt, we hold on to our pain more than we hold onto our joy when we're happy. We allow our peace of mind to be fleeting, but our anger to be everlasting when it should be the other way around. I had to learn how to redirect all the energy I wasted holding the grudge. This scripture in Ephesians sticks out to me, "Get rid of all bitterness, rage and anger, brawling and slander, along with every form of malice." Being angry at her hindered me from healing. It hurt me more than it ever hurt her.

Stop letting others control your emotions. Retaliating against them only turns you into the person that hurt you, do not waste the time and energy. God's vengeance is sufficient.

Self-Reflection: Take a minute to answer the following questions:

- What experience has made you so angry that you harbor resentment and animosity towards someone?
- What do you gain from holding onto the anger you feel for the others who have hurt you?
- What are some things you can gain from letting go of the pain and taking back the power of your emotions?

Suggested Scripture(s):

"Do not rejoice when your enemy falls, and let not your heart be glad when he stumbles." Proverbs 24:17 (ESV)

FIGHTING FEAR

"Fear not, for I am with you; be not dismayed, for I am your God; I will strengthen you, I will help you, I will uphold you with my righteous right hand." Isaiah 41:10 (ESV)

What frightens you? Fear is the worse four letter word you could ever use. What lies are you telling yourself? Have you convinced yourself that you are weak? Do you want to continue your education, but you're afraid that it's too late? Have you opened up a job application, but delay applying because you've told yourself that they would never hire you? Do you have a business burning inside of you, but refuse to move forward? Living in fear is crippling. We need to encourage ourselves to move forward and step out on faith. I see a vision of McCauley Caulkin coming out of the house in Home Alone saying, "I'm not afraid anymore!"

I have always been a water lover. I love to swim. When I was ten-years-old, two of my childhood best friends and I were at the pool in our apartment complex. Each year, we would have to take a swim test to be allowed to get into the deep end of the pool. It was my turn to take my test, so I hopped into the three ft. side of the pool, and waited for the life guard. "You have to swim from this end of the pool to the other side and then back without stopping," the young life guard explained.

"Okay," I said confidently. Why shouldn't I be? I had done the same test several times before. I began my first lap down the distance of the pool. I reached the other side with no problem.

I headed back towards the other end, but halfway through, something strange happened. I came up for air and decided to glance over to look at the lifeguard. To my surprise, he was not looking at me. As a matter of fact, he was not paying attention at all! He had his back to the pool and was talking to someone else. All of a sudden, I got scared. Why wasn't he paying attention to me?

I began to panic and tried to stand up in 6 ft. of water. Once I realized I couldn't stand, I grew even more afraid. I began yelling for help as I bobbed up and down, in and out of the water. The life guard had to jump in and "save me". He pulled me out of the water and to safety. I coughed up some of the water I had swallowed and sat on the side of the pool embarrassed. Other kids chuckled. They were surprised that I was unable to pass the test. Kids half my age had done it with no problem.

After that incident, I stayed away from the deep end of a pool until my freshman year of college. One day, my friends and I were at the pool on campus hanging out and playing around. Someone had the bright idea of everyone jumping off the diving board. My friends started diving in, one after another. When my friend, Devin, noticed that I had not taken a turn yet, he looked at me and said, "Come on, Steph. It's your go." he announced.

"I don't think so," I refuted lying against the rope that separated the deep end and the five ft. end.

"What are you scared of?" he asked with a chuckle.

"Drowning!" I exclaimed.

"You are not going to drown, but to be on the safe side, here," he said as he handed me a floatation belt.

I climbed out of the pool, put on the belt, and adjusted it until it was so tight I could barely breathe. I climbed up on the diving board (the little one) and began my journey to the end. I felt the board began to bend under my felt. I quickly stepped back.

"It's supposed to do that," Devin yelled out to me. I heard him, but I wasn't sure I believed him. Fear began to paralyze me. How deep was this water? Was this belt going to help me float? This questions ran through my mind continuously.

I was so afraid I had not realized that Devin had gotten out of the pool, climbed onto the diving board and stood right next to me!

"What are you doing?" I asked holding on to the rail for dear life.

"I'm going to help you," Devin explained. "We can jump together." The gesture was sweet, but the suggestion made me more nervous than actually jumping itself.

"You go first. Once I watch you, I think I'll feel better," I assured him, although not feeling too sure of that agreement myself. Devin stepped around me, took one leap in the air, and cannonballed into the pool. Everyone cheered and then pointed their attention back to me. Okay, I can do this, I said under my breath. I stepped to the edge, closed my eyes, and jumped! Just like Devin said, I floated back to the top and was safe! I was so proud of myself and so was everyone else. We continued to swim and hang out. After a while, the floatation belt became annoying, so I took it off and swam around in the nine ft. without it. Now, I swim like a fish and jump in the water every chance I get. Although, I'm still not too fond of the diving board!

Growing Pains Life Lessons

We were not created to move in fear. Stop being so concerned about what other people are going to think or say. You do not need the attention of others to accomplish what you set out to do. Stop causing yourself unnecessary fear and anxiety. Trust the process. God will never put you in a situation that He cannot bring you out. We cannot just exist and settle below our potential. Why not cast our cares on God and live our lives to the fullest? Let's exhibit faith and believe that whatever we put our hearts and minds to, we can achieve. Fear is not of God! My church teaches that fear is: False Evidence Appearing Real!

Self-Reflection: Take a moment to answer the following questions

- Has a bad experience turned you away from doing something? If so why?
- What might you gain if you overcame your fear?
- What is something you would do if fear were not standing in your way?

Make a pledge to yourself today to address the things that have caused you to be fearful. I am bigger than my fear. I will not let it consume me. I will _____

Suggested Scripture(s):

"Have I not commanded you? Be strong and courageous. Do not be frightened, and do not be dismayed, for the Lord your God is with you wherever you go." Joshua 1:9(ESV)

"For we walk by faith, not by sight." 2 Corinthians 5:7 (ESV)

CORPORATE AMERICA

"But by the grace of God I am what I am, and his grace toward me was not in vain. On the contrary, I worked harder than any of them, though it was not I, but the grace of God that is with me." 1 Corinthians 15:10 (ESV)

I graduated with a degree in hotel and restaurant management from the University of Maryland Eastern Shore. Our hospitality program was one of the best in the country, so companies visited our campus to recruit upcoming graduates frequently. I had a few job offers upon graduation. I was excited when a prominent hotel chain made me an offer as a Food & Beverage Manager at one of their prestigious properties in Washington, DC. I was ecstatic about graduating a semester early and starting my career with a company I interned with and thought highly of.

I had only been working in my new position for two and half months, when one night we were short staffed, so I helped the restaurant staff during the rush. I was moving a little too fast and hit my right hand on the mahogany bar. I immediately winced in pain. I kept moving, but this time at a slower pace. After a few minutes, I could not ignore the excruciating pain any longer. I went to one of the other managers that I was working with, and he helped me wrap my hand up with a dishcloth and some ice to stop the swelling.

My coworker suggested that I go down to loss prevention to report the incident. I followed his advice and went to file an incident report for my hand. That night, I returned to my room in the hotel and tried to sleep with no hope. I tossed and turned all night. My hand throbbed uncontrollably. The first thing the next morning, I went down to my supervisor's office to tell him what happened, and to inform him I still was not feeling well. To my dismay, my supervisor was nowhere to be found. I returned to loss prevention, and they instructed me to go to the emergency room, so I did. The doctor told me I had sprained my finger and put it in a splint. When I was finally discharged six hours later, I returned to the hotel, to an unhappy supervisor.

"Where have you been?" He questioned.

"At the emergency room," I replied motioning to my hand in the splint just in case he had not noticed it.

"Who told you to go to the emergency room?" he barked.

"Loss prevention," I quietly replied. I was confused by his frustration. Was I not supposed to get my hand looked at?

"Okay, well go change. I need you to be on time. Your shift starts in an hour," he replied irritably.

I went up to my well-decorated hotel room and began to cry. I was exhausted, frustrated, and most of all in pain. I could not believe that my supervisor had been so cold hearted. I pushed through my shift without passing out. I was home resting the next day when the hospital called to inform me that my finger was not sprained but fractured. The doctor instructed me to keep the splint on and follow up with my care physician.

I made a trip to the doctor that week and was told that I would need to go on light duty and stop utilizing my hand for a few weeks to give it a chance to heal. Needless to say, my supervisor was not pleased with the news. He quickly told me that there was no light duty and that I should do the best I could with what I had.

Things were bad for the next few weeks. Little did I know, they were about to get worse. During my follow up with my doctor, they discovered my finger was not getting well. The doctor said he could not understand why it was not healing. I told him that my job did not have light duty and that I still had to work as normal. Since that was the case, he told me that I could not work at all for two weeks! I was surprised, but also a little relieved for the break.

I did not want to call out, so I attended work as scheduled. I sat in our weekly staff meeting and listened intently as my supervisor reviewed the new restaurant menus, and discussed upcoming events. To my surprise, he stopped abruptly and asked,"Ms. Randall, why aren't you taking notes?" I lifted my right hand, which was still wrapped up with a splint on my broken finger.

"Well, write with your other hand," He commanded clearly upset.

"I can't," I rebutted, taken aback by his demeanor and insensitivity.

"Try!" he refuted.

I picked up my pen with my left hand and attempted to scribble the notes as commanded. At that moment, I was embarrassed and frustrated. As a young professional, I did not want to ruffle any feathers. I was working for a major hotel chain, and doing what I loved. I figured I should have been grateful for the opportunity. One side of me felt like maybe I needed to be tougher, while the other part of me knew that it was absurd to be treated with such disrespect.

After the meeting, my supervisor called me into his office. "I want to talk to you about this situation," he said motioning to my hand. "I am going to talk to you like John, and not as your supervisor."

He took off his name badge and placed it on his desk. "You have only been here for a short time," he continued. "You need to suck it up and do what you need to do. I do not care what it takes. If you have to put your arm in a sling and work with one hand, then that's what you need to do." I was in shock at his insensitivity once again. I was uncomfortable with his approach and so-called advice. I told him that I would be taking leave as the doctor had instructed and that I would see him in a few weeks. I got up and walked out of his office.

I was so upset, I wanted to report him to human resources, but why would they believe me? I had only been there a few short months; he had been there for years. He was not only my supervisor but a director. Of course, they would take his word over mine. I felt defeated. When I returned to work, I gave my two weeks' notice. I had found another job that was higher paying, and away from this crazy man.

Growing Pains Life Lessons

I had won, or so I had thought. By removing myself from the situation I thought I was winning, but I was actually doing myself a disservice. In reality, what I had done was allow someone to get away with breaking the law, and potentially repeating the behavior to someone else who would also be afraid of speaking up and reporting him. I missed out on staying with a company that I still to this day love, because of one person. How many times have you walked away from positions and opportunities because you felt mistreated or misunderstood?

When entering into an organization and or company, find out how their processes work, and what the chain of command is. If you feel uncomfortable with the way someone is speaking to you or treating you, find a way to tell that person respectfully the specific behaviors that are bothering you and try to come to a resolution. If you are unable to come to a resolution, seek out a non-biased third party to mediate the situation. Be sure to document all interactions and encounters of inappropriate language.

Seek wise counsel to assist you through the difficult time. Leave resigning as a last resort, and consider all consequences before you do. Let moving on be a choice, not an emergency exit. If you do leave, be sure to give your feedback to your

Human Resources Department, so they can know what to be on the lookout for in the future. Your input could assist them with addressing the issues and concerns of the parties who are still present.

Self-Reflection: Take a moment to answer the following questions

- How can you go about handling difficult people within your company or organization?
- What is your company's protocol on filing grievances about your supervisor?
- Does your company have a no retaliation clause for employees and supervisors, if so what is it?
- What opportunities have you missed out on, because you were afraid to speak up about your feelings or experiences?

Suggested Scripture(s):

"I have fought the good fight, I have finished the race, I have kept the faith" 2 Timothy 4:7(ESV)

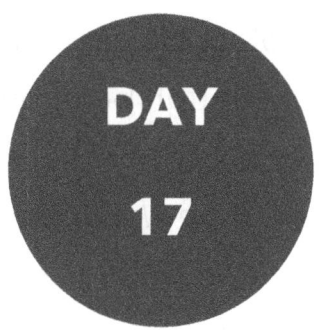

ENVY IS YOUR ENEMY

"They are conceited and understand nothing. They have an unhealthy interest in controversies and quarrels about words that result in envy, strife, malicious talk, evil suspicions." 1 Timothy 6:4 (ESV)

Envy is the one enemy you are allowed to have. If you do not get control of it, it can destroy you. Envy will cause you to idolize people who do not have two pennies to rub together. Envy can cause you to rethink your entire life. It's amazing how an updated status or Instagram pic can change your whole mood with the quickness.

Look at their smiles... I want to be that happy. Look at that ring... I wonder how much it costs? Look at her hair. . . I wish mine were that long. Look at his car. . . I'm still driving around in this bucket. When will enough be enough? When will we get tired of fantasizing over what people want you to see? *"For what shall it profit a man, if he shall gain the whole world, and lose his own soul?" Mark 8:36 (ESV)*

We are so consumed with what other people have. We are never content with what we have been blessed with because we are too focused on what the next person is doing. When we envy others, we tell God that what He has done for us is not enough. We take for granted what He has blessed us with because we are too busy concerning ourselves with what our neighbor has. If you stay in your own lane, there would not be any traffic!

The girl who has what you want is not your enemy. Envy is your enemy. I remember when I dated a guy found attractive by many women. He was educated, had a great job and was a true gentleman. Why am I not married to this catch, you may ask. My answer is simple. On the outside, he appeared to be a catch, but on the inside, he was all over the place. We dated for awhile, but he was very guarded and would not let down his walls.

We went out frequently, but our conversations were subpar at best. He was very lackluster. He was a social butterfly around is his friends and even mine, but one-on-one, there was no real chemistry. His actions did not match his word. Although he was a "good guy", I knew he was not the right man for me. We remained friends on social media, and I would just be so entertained by how females gushed over him and vied for his attention. They were so jealous of what they THOUGHT I was getting. They envied what we had. Instead of wondering why I would let " a catch" go, they were just happy he was back on the market.

When we use others to measure how great our lives are, how successful we are, or how attractive we are, we give society the power to say whether or not we are sufficient based on their standards and not God's. Social media is the core of this issue because of the people who misuse them. You can't make an assumption about people's lives based on a few clicks of a camera.

Most of the time, people have something I call "Closet Envy." It is not obvious, and they would deny it if you called them out on it. It can be your family or friends, and sometimes it can even be your significant other. People want what you have even if they won't admit it. You could be a waitress making $5.00 an hour, working 12 hours a day, and someone who makes five times what you do, with a nice car and expensive shoes will walk in, see how beautiful you are and feel a tinge of jealousy.

I have a friend I think is beautiful inside and out. She's educated, gorgeous, and has a great family support system. She has been afforded opportunities other people could only even dream of, but she is still not 100% happy with herself. Now in retrospect to most women her age, I could not understand her frustration until I saw her interact with some of her other friends.

To me, she is slim and beautiful, but compared to other friends in her circle, she could stand to lose a few pounds. To me, she appeared to be financially secure, but she wanted to purchase red bottoms without having to check her bank account like some of her friends were fortunate enough to do. Needless to say, I was surprised that someone others envied did not think she had it all together. She still felt some things were unattainable, and in turn envied her friends who lived the lifestyle she desired to have.

Growing Pains Life Lessons

There is always something someone is going to have or do that is going to be better than us. This is the way of life. If we were all made the same, that would be a boring existence. It is okay to show admiration for the accomplishments of others, but do not allow it to consume you to the point where you cannot be happy with what you have. Envy will not get you any closer to what someone else has. What is meant for you, is just for you. If someone else has it, that just means something better is in store for you. Do not allow admiration to turn into aggravation!

Self-Reflection: Take a moment to answer the following questions

- What area of your life are you seeking elevation from God (i.e. career, finances, love)?
- How has envy changed your relationship with a friend or family member?

Suggested Scripture(s):

"You desire but do not have, so you kill. You covet but you cannot get what you want, so you quarrel and fight. You do not have because you do not ask God." James 4:2 (ESV)

DAY 18

DATING & WAITING

"Do not be anxious about anything, but in everything by prayer and supplication with thanksgiving let your requests be made known to God. And the peace of God, which surpasses all understanding, will guard your hearts and your minds in Christ Jesus." Philippians 4:6-7(ESV)

Most of us have the dating part down pact, but struggle with the waiting. Contrary to popular belief, it can be a struggle for women just like it is for men. Now I am not saying that women feel the same; however between our hormones and emotions, waiting for Mr. Right can feel like an eternity. Most (not all) women have a strong desire to be married and to have children. As you go through your life, the responses you get in your twenties are not quite the same responses you receive in your thirties and forties.

In my early twenties, people always told me I had all the time in the world to get married. "Focus on you and your career right now; you're still young." They would say. Once I got into my late twenties, and early thirties and more of my friends started to get married and or have children people began to say "What are you waiting for?" When you are single, you are bombarded with questions and suggestions of what you need to do to get your husband or wife.

Everyone has an opinion of what you should be doing, and sometimes one contradicts the other. We feel overwhelmed with the pressure of society, our family and friends. We are so concerned with living to satisfy others that we do not take the time out to figure out who or what we really want. Most of the time their advice is given in love, but it does not make it sting any less when you've been praying for the very thing someone else is judging you for not having.

I use to get frustrated with the dozens of questions and comments that were thrown at me until I became at peace with my decision to do things "the right way". Most of those people did not realize that I was not being a monk. I dated, loved, and lost, but I did not wait. Like many others, I wanted what I wanted, when I wanted it. I did things my way to get where I thought I wanted to be.

I had a mental checklist of what I wanted my man to be. After a few months of dating, if things went well we would progress into a physical relationship, but none of those relationships ended in marriage. That is not the goal of dating and waiting. The waiting portion is not to be based on a scale of how many dates you have gone on, how many months or years you have dated or even your feelings. There is only one expiration date when it comes to dating and waiting, and that is your wedding day!

The dating portion of a friendship and even a relationship is to determine if you can see yourself with this person for the rest of your life. Do your goals, morals, and purposes align, or is it solely just based on the physical attraction and or material things?

When dating, we need to view the person pursing us through sober eyes. When dating someone, do not date just for your right now, date for your future. We ignore the small things that bother us about people instead of determining if those things will ultimately be deal breakers. We cannot be consumed with potential and not focus on measuring progress. We pray about jobs, finances, and even material things, but we do not seek God about the person we wish to be with for the rest of our lives. How is that be possible?

Dating is about you finding out what you are looking for in a potential mate. That is why it is important to leave out intimacy. Physical connections cause soul ties that can confuse what you feel about a person. Once you build that connection and bond, it is harder to walk away from someone who may not be a good fit for you, because your judgment is clouded. Do not complicate your ability to distinguish if the person you are interested in is someone just for now or someone God has ordained for the rest of your life.

Everyone is not the one. That was the biggest obstacle I had to overcome when it came to waiting on God to bless me with my husband. I saw everyone as a potential mate. If I met a man at the grocery store and he was cute and had a great sense of humor, I started to wonder if he could be "the one." I did not even know his last name, if he was a Christian, or if he was even straight. Every time you allow your flesh to be the measure of how you are going to entertain the people you meet, you do yourself a disservice. You are pretty much saying, "I am going to settle for what I can get instead of waiting for what I want." It is all a test. How bad do you want the real thing?

Work on building a friendship first. Every good relationship is built on a good friendship. Just because someone is a good man or woman does not mean that they are necessarily good for you. I cannot tell you how many times I have met a really good guy who was a great friend, but when we crossed over into dating, the relationship went sour. You should be in prayer about the things you want in a partner. God will fulfill His promise and give you what is in His will. Trust that God knows us better than we know ourselves. He knows the desire of our hearts spoken and unspoken.

While you are dating, it is important to have a good accountability partner who can encourage and support you through your journey. Ensure that it is someone who shares your same faith and values. It does not help to go to your friends and family who do not believe in your process. You need someone who can speak life into your situation, and hold you accountable to do things the right way. You do not want to have a yes man as your accountability partner. They will not be able to be firm and honest with you which is an imperative part of being held accountable.

In addition to your accountability partner, the person you need to be honest with is you. If you know you are not prepared to date without intimacy or jumping into one bad relationship after another; you may need to be in isolation. Take some time and shut down the dating. Do not call, text, date, or hang out with someone of the opposite sex. If that means you have to block people or delete numbers, do what it takes to get refocused. You have to think of what is at stake in the long run, and not just your temporary feelings. It is not going to be easy, but I promise it will be worth it.

Growing Pains Life Lessons

Set your boundaries and stick to them. Only you know your weaknesses. If you are not strong enough to be alone without caving into temptation, try to hang out in groups and do not spend private time alone. It is important to choose your words carefully. I am very flirtatious, so when I talk to a guy I am interested in, I limit my flirtation and do my part to keep the conversation from going left. My mentor/accountability partner also advised me to cut out those late night, in the bed conversations. Being in bed made me put down my inhibitions and get too comfortable.

Date with purpose. Do not waste your time if you do not see long-term potential. Create a list of deal breakers, and learn how to apply the 80/20 rule. If someone has 80% of what you want, it is okay to move forward as long as your essential needs and wants are met with. No one is going to be perfect, but they should be perfect for you!

Self-Reflection: Take a moment to answer the following questions

- What is your definition of dating?

- What standards do you have in place to maintain boundaries when dating?

- Write a note to your current/ future partner on your expectations for courtship.

- How can you move forward without making the same mistakes, as you have with past relationships?

Suggested Scripture(s):

"I believe that I shall look upon the goodness of the Lord in the land of the living! Wait for the Lord; be strong, and let your heart take courage; wait for the Lord!" Psalm 27:13-14 (ESV)

GUILTY BY ASSOCIATION

"But now I am writing to you not to associate with anyone who bears the name of brother if he is guilty of sexual immorality or greed, or is an idolater, reviler, drunkard, or swindler—not even to eat with such a one." 1 Corinthians 5:11(ESV)

We sometimes struggle with distancing ourselves from people who do not reflect our core values. It's hard to be friends with a drug addict without people thinking you divulge in drugs as well. Unfortunately, I did not consider that while I was dealing with Travis. The first time he walked into the Real Estate office where I worked, I was intrigued. Travis was a friend of my coworker, and to my surprise, he inquired about me and asked for my number. Now I am pretty and have a great personality, but his type was usually not interested in "good girls".

Travis and I talked and texted for two weeks, but had not seen each other since our first encounter. One night, my roommate and my cousin from out of town were coming back from a night out in DC. While we were at the train station waiting for a cab, he called. I told him we were going to take a taxi home, but he insisted on coming to pick us up. I agreed, and we waited for him to arrive at the station. Moments later, he called my cell to say that he was at the station. I looked around in confusion since I had not seen a car enter the station.

I asked where he was, and he honked. I looked up and saw that he had pulled up in the back part of the station. I told him that we would walk across to the lot where he was. Before we could cross the street, I saw his car drive up onto the sidewalk and across to where we were standing. I laughed in shock. My roommate, my cousin and I jumped into the back seat. "You're crazy," I announced. He screeched out of the station and headed past the car dealerships. As we turned onto Branch Avenue, flashing lights lit up the inside of the car from the rear.

I turned to look out the back window and saw the police lights behind us. Oh no, I said to myself. Travis pulled the car over. We sat there for several minutes, but the officer did not approach the car. Just then, he checked his rearview mirror and announced. "It's just the metro station police. If I had known it wasn't the real police, I would've kept going," He laughed. I breathed a sigh of relief, but a moment too soon.

Just then, I heard sirens as four police cars surrounded the front, left, and rear of our car. The officers came to the car with their weapons drawn. They screamed for us to put our hands up and get out of the car. Travis and his friend descended out of the front, while my roommate, my cousin and I climbed out of the back of the car. My heart was beating a mile a minute. An officer told me to put my hands behind my back and proceeded to put handcuffs on me. I burst out in tears as he sat me on the curb, and proceeded to do the same with my cousin, and roommate. They took Travis and put him in the back of one of the police cars.

One of the officers approached me and told me to calm down. He informed me that I was not in trouble, but were being detained to be sure we did not run. He picked me up and removed the cuffs from me and the other girls. He asked where we lived, and I gave him our address. He said that he would drop us off. I asked what would happen to Travis, and he told me I should not be concerned about him. I told him that I felt bad because I had gotten him into trouble when he was trying to do us a favor and take us home. The officer quickly got frustrated and said, "No, it is not your fault. He was driving reckless, and he had someone else's tags on his car." I was surprised. He asked if he was my boyfriend, and I told him he was an acquaintance.

He said, " Good! You seem like a nice girl. Stay away from that guy."

I heard what he said, but I was not listening. If I had only listened to that police officer, I would have been saved from a year and a half of drama, heartache and pain. I had never been in trouble with the police before, and within the first ten minutes of being in the guy's company, I was being detained. God will send a message in many shapes and forms, but will we listen before it is too late? How much clearer could he have been? He waved a big red flag: DANGER DO NO ENTER! Instead of running far away from him, I did the opposite and became his girlfriend. It was all fun in games until things like joy, peace, and money started to come up missing.

A little over a year had passed since Travis and I had met. I went away to school and broke up with him. He was like a drug for me, and I needed to go to rehab quick! Going away to college was my saving grace, but just like any drug addict, I thought I could just have one hit now and then without it affecting me. I came home for spring break and called him just to say hi. He asked if we could hang out and I quickly agreed. He came to pick me up, and the attraction was still there. He had a fresh haircut, his cologne smelled amazing, and he was dressed in a black polo shirt, Gucci shoes, and Gucci jeans. We went to meet up with my cousin and her boyfriend at a hotel nearby. We all laughed, talked and hung out. It got late, so my cousin said that we could crash there with them.

We woke up early the next morning, and I knew that I needed to get back to my friend's house. My cousin and her boyfriend were still sleeping, so we left out quietly. As we were walking out, Travis paused and said he needed to go to the bathroom. He gave me the keys and told me to go to the car. I obliged and headed to the car. The car ride home was quiet but normal. He kissed me goodbye, and I went into the house.

I hadn't been in the house for five minutes before my cousin called my cell phone. I answered, and she was hysterical. She said that $200.00 was missing out of her boyfriend's pants' pocket. I was in shock. I quickly told her that I did not know what happened to the money. She asked if I was with Travis the whole time. I said yes, but then I remembered he went back into the room to "use the bathroom." I quickly realized that there was a chance he had stolen the money.

I felt sick to my stomach. My cousin's boyfriend felt like it had been a setup. I couldn't believe it. I was a self-proclaimed good girl who worked two jobs, and a first-year college student. How was I being called a thief? I apologized repeatedly and assured her I had nothing to do with it.

"It does not matter, he's your friend," she rebutted. I felt awful and helpless. She was absolutely right. I had brought someone untrustworthy into her space. He had proven that to me time and time again, but I had chosen to overlook the obvious. Not only had I been naïve, but now I had been lumped in with someone who was a thief.

Growing Pains Life Lessons

How can we walk alongside someone who does not have the same moral compass and values as we do and expect it not to affect us? "Whoever walks with the wise becomes wise, but the companion of fools will suffer harm." Proverbs 13:20. None of us are without sin or fault, but if we are not showing remorse and repenting our actions, we are committing to go against what is right. All my family and friends are not saved, but that does not mean I love them any less. I just know what boundaries I need to set within those relationships.

I will not go shopping with someone who is a kleptomaniac, and I will not go to a bar with an alcoholic. I am not going to engage or support their toxic behaviors. Sometimes that means I have to love them from afar. Encourage them and support them as much as you can, but do not allow them to drag you into their bondage. *"Blessed is the man who walks not in the counsel of the wicked, nor stands in the way of sinners, nor sits in the seat of scoffers;" Psalm 1:1 (ESV)*

I went home for the summer two months later, and someone at work told me that Travis had been killed in an accident. He was 23. I was devastated. I cried for weeks. Somehow, I felt like I had failed him. I thought that if I had stayed in contact with him, tried harder, and prayed more, I could have saved him. At the time, I did not understand how crazy that sounded. We belong to the King of Kings and the Lord of Lords. He died so that we may be saved. Travis had to make a decision to be saved.

We take too much responsibility for other people's actions. God gives us all free will. We have to choose how we want to live our lives. Sometimes, we do not always make the best choices, but it is our conscious decision. I was sad that this young man would never get the opportunity to turn his life around, but if I had stayed with him, there was a good chance I would have ruined my life.

You become the company that you keep. Your reputation is judged by the people you are seen with. It may not be fair or realistic, but that is the reality. You have to be strong enough to speak up if someone is doing or saying something around you that goes against what you stand for. If that person respects you enough, they will take heed. If not, you need to make the best decision for you. Even if you are not committing infractions, you condone them by not rectifying the situation.

Self-Reflection: Take a moment to answer the following questions

- Who are you socializing with that could damage your reputation?
- What have you done to help friends or family turn away from bad behaviors?
- Moving forward, how are you going to address things that go against what you believe?
- How can you love and respect others without going against your morals and values?

Suggested Scripture(s):

"Do not be deceived: Bad company ruins good morals." 1 Corinthians 15:33 (ESV)

"Can a man carry fire next to his chest and his clothes not be burned?" Proverbs 6:27 (ESV)

WE WEAR THE MASKS

"For you formed my inward parts; you knitted me together in my mother's womb. I praise you, for I am fearfully and wonderfully made. Wonderful are your works; my soul knows it very well." Psalm 139:13-14 (ESV)

Have you ever asked someone how they were doing, and they gave you a weak smile and a short "good"? I know I have. Do we ever stop to think how we really feel before we answer those questions? Of course, not. After all, who wants to hear the truth? Who wants to know that you are stressed out, your husband did not come home last night, your parents are ill, or you are behind on your bills? We walk around as if everything is swell. We put on our best clothes, drive our expensive cars, brag about our latest conquests, but underneath the "mask" we are not whole. We are barely keeping it together.

I had a mentee named Oscar. He was eighteen. He had moved from New Jersey, but his parents were from Ghana. His parents were very strict. Oscar, he was extremely proper and articulate. He always had very nice clothes, and shoes. Oscar had received college offers from several Ivy League schools. He was a very intelligent young man with a bright future. Sometimes his peers would get frustrated with him and tease him because he appeared to have it all. Some thought he acted as if he was better than them. He did not waste time going to parties or focusing on girls like his counterparts. He was determined to get a great education and become a doctor.

A few months before graduation, Oscar began to change. At first, it was a very subtle. I didn't notice the change in his demeanor until he lashed out at me for a not being available to meet with him as I promised. I was caught off-guard by how angry he was. I had never seen him upset before. I apologized and told him that I would meet with him at our next scheduled time. When I arrived at the school the next week, I was surprised to hear from one of the counselors that Oscar had been caught smoking marijuana. This was not the Oscar I knew. When I asked him about the incident, he said that some of his classmates were smoking in the stairwell and talked him into trying it. When I talked to him, he seemed remorseful and promised never to try it again.

I chalked it up to him being a curious teenager and moved on from the incident. I hoped we would never have to talk about drugs again. Unfortunately, three weeks later Oscar went home intoxicated. Although his parents didn't catch him, he confessed to me. Again, he seemed very aware that he had made a stupid mistake. I told him to stay on track and not allow these things to jeopardize his future. He was only a few months away from graduation. To my surprise,

Oscar called me one night at 11 p.m. He sounded unlike himself and very upset. He was overwhelmed with his classes, frustrated with his recent actions, and overwhelmed with the pressure of having to maintain his perfect image. He also confessed that he had shut down and started to slack off on his assignments. I advised him to take a step back, refocus, and try to take things one day at a time. I suggested that he reach out to his teachers about the assignments he had missed, and speak to his counselor and parents about how he was feeling. He agreed to try to make up the work and speak to a counselor but said that his parents' culture was very different. He felt like they would not understand. I told Oscar that I could see how his senior year and getting ready for college could be overwhelming, and urged him to journal and continue to talk to us about what was going on.

Then, I did something that I had never done with a mentee or student outside of church. I asked Oscar if I could pray with him. He quickly said yes. As I prayed, I could hear Oscar began to cry. In the end, I asked if he was okay. He reassured me that he felt much better. I was relieved to hear that and prayed that our conversation got him back on track. Sadly, my relief did not last for long.

I was out of town when I received a devastating phone call that Oscar had tried to commit suicide by taking a handful of pills. Luckily, someone found him in time. The ambulance was able to get him to the hospital in time to pump his stomach. Sadness washed over me, and I began to cry. I felt that I had failed Oscar. I should have talked to him more, or gone with him to the counselor. I did not realize how deeply he had fallen into depression. How could I have not known? I worked with students all the time, and I was trained on suicide response. I honestly did not anticipate him trying to take his life. The suicide attempt was a wake-up call for me, as well as, Oscar's parents. They removed him from school for the remainder of the school year and got him into counseling. He returned to school the next year, graduated and went to a local college.

I had to reflect overtime and consider all the things I have encountered throughout my life up until this point. I tried to confess my thoughts and fears to those closest to me, but I was shut down or misunderstood. Just like Oscar, I did not want to be judged by those around me. I didn't want people to know that I struggled with the things of my past.

Growing Pains Life Lessons

I had to learn that it is okay not to be okay. It is acceptable to admit when we are hurting, worried, lonely, etc. Unfortunately, covering up things is an emotion we learned as children. Growing up, many of us have heard our parents say, "What happens in this house, stays in this house. It is no one else's business." What about when what is happening in your head or at your home is killing you? It's time to say no to the secrets, and no to pretending that things are okay. As millennials, we will not pass those bad habits to the next generation.

We need to be in tune with ourselves and our Heavenly Father. The one person I could never hide from was God; He could see right through me. My heart became so heavy that I had no choice except to confess my burdens to Him. He then put my amazing mentor, Niyonu, into my life. She poured into me and guided me through the rough times. She was truly a godsend!

I urge you to look at the red flags that may come up with friends and family. Have their demeanor or habits changed? If you notice people are starting to go into isolation or shy away from things they were once passionate about, reach out and offer them a listening ear. Pray for them, and encourage them to pray on their own. People have a negative connotation about seeking counseling or therapy, but it can be beneficial to speak to a non-bias person and share what you may not be comfortable telling your friends or family. Whatever you do, don't suffer in silence.

Self-Reflection: Take a moment to answer the following questions

- Who can you be transparent with?
- What do you think would happen if you were honest about how you feel?
- Do you feel the need to wear a mask and pretend you are something or someone that you are not? If so, why?

Suggested Scripture(s)

"Beloved, do not believe every spirit, but test the spirits to see whether they are from God, for many false prophets have gone out into the world." 1 John 4:1(ESV)

"And after you have suffered a little while, the God of all grace, who has called you to his eternal glory in Christ, will himself restore, confirm, strengthen, and establish you." 1 Peter 5:10 (ESV)

ALONE & NOT LONELY

"O Lord, all my longing is before you; my sighing is not hidden from you." Psalm 38:9 (ESV)

Growing up as an only child, I hated being alone. I never got the memo about creating an imaginary friend, so I was adamant about seeking the attention of others. There is power in the ability to be alone. If you do not get to a private space, how can you spend time with God and make yourself available to hear what He wants to tell you? We have to be comfortable with ourselves.

We cannot live for others if we do not understand our purpose. God wants to use us. He can only use us if we allow him to. It is important to do the work and put in the effort to grow and develop. Why do you feel uncomfortable being alone? What void are you trying to fill? Learning how to enjoy your own company is a must. Waiting on others to experience happiness is not realistic. When we depend on others for our happiness, we develop a dependency on others to bring us joy. What happens when that person leaves? We are not able to receive that same happiness, so we find ourselves in a state of loneliness.

Being my mother's only child, I always craved the company of others. I became bored easily. I wanted someone to play with and talk to other than my mother. Through most of college, I had roommates and enjoyed the experience (most of the time). I liked having someone around to talk to and hang out. It was convenient to have people close by, but I quickly learned we still had different lives, schedules, and friends which meant they were not always available when I wanted them to be. When I was 25, I changed jobs and finally had my own space. Once I had my own space, I realized how much I enjoyed being on my own. I had the choice of when I wanted to be around people, and when I needed some me time.

I hung out with my coworkers a lot because of the nature of our job and hours we worked. Most of my friends outside of my job had opposing schedules to mine, which meant I would wait for weeks just for our schedules to match up to go see a movie. Half of the time, it would be too late, and I'd have to wait to catch it on Redbox. Eventually, I discovered that I did not always have to have other people around to do the things I enjoyed. I began to enjoy my own company so much, I didn't bother asking if someone wanted to go with me. I was afraid that their schedule would delay my desire.

I didn't want my experiences to be based on others. Even now, I go to brunch and enjoy the comfort of being able to be alone. Most people enjoy having a gym accountability partner. Not me. I was a spontaneous person. I liked being able to go to the gym at eight a.m. or eleven p.m. if I wanted. Sometimes, waiting on others can become a crutch for you. If my gym partner were not able to make it, I would probably have to skip my gym time just to wait for them. That would only be doing a disservice to myself. We have to be able to push and motivate ourselves. We have to take care of ourselves mentally, physically, emotionally, and most important, spiritually. I love to attend the 12 o'clock service at church. I do not mind sitting alone, and technically I'm not because there are thousands of people around me. I have peace when I can go to church, get a word, and even meet new people. If I waited for others to attend church with me, I wouldn't enjoy the experience as much.

Travel alone, eat alone, go to the movies, do whatever it is your heart desires. Now that doesn't mean you should become anti-social. Don't go back and tell your friends and family that I said you don't need them!

While you're out enjoying life, do not forget to make time for God. Not just the quick prayer we do at night before going to bed or saying grace over a meal. I'm talking about frequent, intentional time with God. I learned that when I began carving out time for Him every day, my days became more manageable. I encourage you to do the same. Read daily devotionals. Pray about your day, ask for guidance, and thank Him for what He has already done. Pray for a hedge of protection around your family and loved one. Pray for your pastors, friends, family, and neighbors. These are just a few things you can do in your time with God.

Growing Pains Life Lessons

Isolation can be the devil's playgrounds if not used wisely. The difference between being alone and isolation is choice. Being alone can be for a few hours or just taking a break to enjoy some quiet time. Being in isolation is a continuous act of closing yourself off from the world for an undetermined amount of time. We must have balance. It is unhealthy to feel that you will die without someone in your life. It is okay to desire companionship. This becomes a problem when you depend on their companionship for happiness.

When you are feeling lonely or overwhelmed, talk to God. He is always there. He knows everything that you think and feel, but take the time to be transparent with Him. Your prayer could be, "Lord, I feel lonely. I have a void that only you can fill. Please provide me with your comfort, love and peace."

Even when we are in relationships, married, or have children, we still need to have a quiet place and be able to have some "me time". That is an important part of our relationships. We need time to be alone with our thoughts and recharge. Make time to quiet the world and tap into your needs.

Self-Reflection: Take a moment to answer the following questions:

- Do you have a constant need to be around others? If so, why?
- What are some things that you have not done because you are waiting on others?
- What activities can you try solo?
- How can you balance your quiet time and hanging with friends and family?

Suggested Scripture(s):

"Be strong and courageous. Do not fear or be in dread of them, for it is the Lord your God who goes with you. He will not leave you or forsake you." Deuteronomy 3:16 (ESV)

TUNNEL VISION

"And the Lord answered me: "Write the vision; make it plain on tablets, so he may run who reads it." Habakkuk 2:2 (ESV)

Every year, I would create a vision board of the things I sought to accomplish. Sometimes, God's plans are different from our own, so I was sure to consult with Him before I planned and created my vision board. Making a vision board helped me to clarify, concentrate and maintain focus on specific life goals. Looking at the images that represented what I wanted to be and accomplish motivated me.

Growing up, I was focused on getting a "good job" and making enough money to live comfortably. The only P word I was concerned about was passion. I wanted to make good money doing something I was passionate about. Over the years, those things changed frequently. I wanted to be a chef, a professor, and an author. I was passionate about everything I did, but I had not considered which of my passions God had created me to do. I struggled with trying to decide what was next. I started on a journey to find a career that did more than pay the bills.

As I began to talk to my friends and mentors, they approached me with a P word that I had not given much consideration. That word was purpose! What's your purpose? They all asked. I would poke out my chest and open my mouth wide, but then a strange thing occurred. I became speechless. I could not formulate the words. I felt my purpose was teaching and hospitality. That is where my strengths and passion were, but then I also loved writing. It was what I had always aspired to do. I knew that it had to be my purpose, so I started to do the work to make sure.

I never wanted to be stumped by that question again. I had major pride issues, so being unable to articulate my purpose was too much to handle. I had to find out what my purpose was, and if I had been walking in it. *"And we know that for those who love God all things work together for good, for those who are called according to his purpose." Romans 8:28 (ESV)*

I began taking online quizzes and praying about it. I learned what my spiritual gifts were, and began to walk in the direction of my purpose. God also let me in on a secret. Your calling and your purpose can change for different seasons of your life. I was in a ministry I loved, but I knew that I had to push myself to do even more. God was calling me to lend my talents and skills in other areas. He charged me with the task to do more outreach and testify to those who have experienced struggles similar to my own.

Life is so much sweeter when we serve with a servant's heart instead of pushing our agendas. I read The Purpose Driven Life in a book club with some of my Queen Esther sisters, and it opened my eyes. My best friend, Fatima, often said she did not understand how I could take on so much at one time. I worked full time, was an aspiring author, had started a small catering business, was active in church, and taught one to two courses. She jokingly shared that she was so tired after work, all she wanted to do was rest. I thought back to the days of having a 9-5 position without additional responsibilities. I felt empty. I could not imagine not doing the additional things I do now.

Growing Pains Life Lessons

There was a simple reason why Fatima and I felt so differently about the number of hours in a day. God had given us two different visions, and two different purposes. One was no better than the other; they were just different. The same is for all of us. We all have different purposes.

I was in the middle of writing a fictional novel when God stopped me and put this book in my heart. When I became obedient to the things He instructed me to do, things shifted for me. He gave me a renewed sense of hope. He gave me peace. My tears of sadness became tears of joy and wholeness. Have you ever served God? I do not mean going to church and helping out when the pastor asks. I mean really serving God? When we serve God, our posture, mindsets, and attitudes are completely different than when we serve man.

He showed me that I had not endured life's circumstances in vain. He had allowed everything to lead me to healing and wholeness. God had prepared me for my purpose. He made me more in tune with those around me to see what they were in need of physically, spiritually, and financially. When we set your minds on serving God and not man things, bother us less. We stop worrying about our finances, careers, family, and futures because we know God will provide what we need. Sometimes, it's difficult to blindly follow God, especially when we have our desired way of doing things. Our peace is in knowing that what we are doing is in His will. Do not allow others to distract or discourage you, because you are resting on the promises He has made you.

Self-Reflection: Take a moment to answer the following questions and complete the activity.

- What have you blamed on others?

- What has God put on your heart to do? How will you accomplish it?

- What is hindering you in your journey?

- Take time out to create a vision board of the things you would like to accomplish in the next six months.

Suggested Scripture(s):

"The Lord will fulfill his purpose for me; your steadfast love, O Lord, endures forever. Do not forsake the work of your hands." Psalm 138:8 (ESV)

MARRIAGE IS THE MOTIVE

"I woke up with a wide smile today, waiting for all the wonderful things he'll say. The new things he has planned just for me, the promise of how wonderful his comfort will be. This is always the best part of my day, sitting in quiet so you can have your way. I close my eyes and go bended knee. My Morning Prayer time when God expresses his unconditional love for me."

-"Meet Him in the Morning" by Stephanie L. Randall

Love is such an amazing gift in its purest form. Once we learn love's intended purpose, we no longer take it for granted or use it as a pawn. How much do you love yourself? I mean real unconditional love. We have a tendency to let our love waiver depending on our feelings. God's love is unconditional. We cannot earn it, and we cannot lose it. He gives it to us of His own free will. We should give and receive that same unconditional love from others. Unconditional love is not based on what we have, or what we can do. If we love based on circumstance, our love would change daily.

You're visible, but are you available? You can go places, events, and see people at church. They see you, but they aren't looking at you. They can't pick up on the fact that you're spiritually or emotionally unavailable. I was at a point in life where I felt I needed to be single and not have any involvement with men. Even though I was unavailable, I would still get approached. My old coworker, now my brother in Christ, finally explained to me that although I said I did not want anyone to approach me, there was something in my posture and attitude that gave off a vibe that I was available. I valued his honesty and learned that I needed to change who I was because I didn't like who I was attracting.

It is imperative to learn how to be happy in your singleness. I know that it is easier said than done. I was a serial monogamous. I loved to be in relationships. That was my secure place, even though insecurities were birthed out of them. I did not know how to be alone. Even when I was single, I was not alone. I had males that I would still text, call or go out on dates. I would justify my actions by saying, I'm not committed to anyone, I'm just "doing me". The truth was relationships were a crutch for me. I used them to fill a void that stemmed from my childhood, but it took me years to acknowledge and address the issue.

You cannot go into any situation still broken from your last. It is not fair to you or your future spouse. What is the real reason you want to be married? If it's for the sake of changing your last name, wearing a flashy ring on your finger, impressing others or having someone to sleep with at night, you are not ready to be a wife. What qualifies you to be a wife? You can cook, you're clean, and you go to church. Those things are great but do not necessarily make you a wife. God creates and instills attributes in us as women that we tap into when we get serious about God, His house and the sanctity of marriage.

You cannot hear from God and receive what He has for you if you are always surrounded by an entourage. The one could show up, but to you, they are just another face in the crowd, because all the wrong ones are blocking your view. In the meantime, God wants to use you. Use your time to build your relationship with God. He wants you to fulfill the purpose He has designed for you in your singleness. If you want to get married, you have to be in preparation. You have to be whole before you can be someone's other half. If you are looking for someone to complete you, draw closer to God. He is the only one who can fill that order.

Save yourself the heartache and pain and do the work before you try to be with someone else. A mate should be a compliment to you, not a supplement. What do you mean, Stephanie? I mean your partner should be able to support you in your vision and ministry. They should have the same morals and beliefs when it comes to family. They should share in your ideas and dreams. You should not be looking for a partner to help you afford a certain lifestyle, make you feel complete, or make you feel loved. If you get with someone because you feel like something is missing, you will always feel like that. I know you think that is impossible but just think about it. If you marry someone contingent upon what they can do for you, what will you do if they can no longer do it?

Growing Pains Life Lessons

Marriage is a lot of work. It is not about what someone can do for you, but more so what you both can do for the Kingdom of God. Some would actually consider marriage a calling because it takes a special type of person to be able to submit, love, and honor another person. If you are dating or in a courtship with someone, seek a successful married couple for mentorship. It is important to receive wise counsel before making a lifetime commitment. Take advantage of your church's pre-marital course to get more insight. Ensure that you and your significant other are on the same page.

My church has a phenomenal pre-marital program which consists of two courses "So you think you want to get married" and "Becoming One." I know several people who have gone through the processes and spoke highly of the content and programs. For more information, please visit our church's website at www.fbcglenarden.org.

Self-Reflection: Take a moment to answer the following questions

- What do you believe the purpose of marriage is?
- What can you do to prepare for and or maintain a healthy marriage?

Suggested Scripture(s):

"So they are no longer two, but one flesh. Therefore what God has joined together, let no one separate." Matthew 19:6 (ESV)

Lost in Lust

By: Stephanie L. Randall

I crave you like a cup of coffee after a long night, I think of you when I wake up in the morning and before I go to bed at night.

When am I going to see you? I know it's only been a few hours, but when you're not here your love loses its power

These decisions have me tied up too tight; blurring the lines so I can't tell wrong from right,

Hours turn into days, missed calls and unanswered texts; trying to figure out why I haven't why I haven't heard from you when you told me I was the best.

So a month later I lay here alone, replaying everything that happened and questioning where I went wrong.

I thought you were my godsend, a man who could talk to me hours; you said you wanted to be my lover and friend, but it was only me that you wanted to devour

If I was your wife wouldn't you have done it right and dedicated your life? ; But instead I'm just sitting here remembering the night you said hello, realizing there's no other place to go

But then again I end up in sin again, wondering why God did I let lust lead me here again.

To this dead end road where happily ever after does not exist, but misery and soul ties are all that this really is.

LOST IN LUST

"But I say, walk by the Spirit, and you will not gratify the desires of the flesh." Galatians 5:16 (ESV)

You would be surprised at what lust would make you do. It can make you throw out all your inhibitions and even worse, your morals. Attraction is an important part of dating. You want to have a certain amount of chemistry with the person you are with. What was it that attracted you to your current or previous partner? Was it their eyes, smile, or physique? While attraction is an important part, it should not be the glue that holds your relationship together.

If you cannot stand the sound of their voice, cannot agree with the lifestyle they lead or are displeased with the way they treat others, you should reconsider what is keeping you there. Many times I ignored the signs that were as large as a billboard on the side of the road. Do you ever wonder why people always say, "If I knew then what I know now?" It's a true statement. When you do not have your blinders on, you are unable to make sound decisions without your heart or hormones in the way.

I had fallen in lust before and confused it with love. I dated a guy I thought was the one. We talked for several months before becoming exclusive. When we were together, he made me feel incredible. He was sweet, funny, and affectionate. Although I wanted to wait, there was something about him that made me weak when we were apart. He was a horrible communicator and sometimes acted like a totally different person.

I was so frustrated. I knew I deserved better. Every other week, I would say I was going to break it off, but when we finally got face-to-face, I couldn't resist him and believed him when he said he would do better. Weeks turned into months and months turned into a year. I was still unhappy, but our physical relationship made me weak mentally and emotionally. I did not like how I felt when I was with him. I hated that he had so much power over me. I finally broke away, blocked his number, and started to get back to myself spiritually.

Are you confusing lust with love? The word says God is love. If we do not believe in God, we cannot truly know how to love. When we create sexual soul ties, we begin to blur the lines and get confused. The temporary euphoria we feel makes us think it's love when it's really lust.

Growing Pains Life Lessons

Make sure that people are who they say they are. Do their actions and words align? Their words are who they want to be, but their actions show who they truly are. Doing the same thing over and over again and expecting different results is the definition of insanity. When we continue to take the same course of action time after time, we need to stop and see where the break down is. We know that every time we have sex with someone we are not committed to, we are going to eventually start feeling guilty. So how do we break the cycle?

We must first learn that after a mistake is repeated, it goes from being a mistake to being a choice. What we choose forms who we are becoming. Make the choice to wait. Don't allow yourself to be sold on who a person says they are. Take the time out to learn who they truly are.

Self-Reflection: Take a moment to complete the following activity.

Take a sheet of paper and write the attributes you desire from your current or future mate. Make two columns. Label one column Lust and the other Love. Take the attributes that you listed and write each one under the relevant column. Does the love outweigh the lust?

Suggested Scripture(s):

"For this is the will of God, your sanctification: that you abstain from sexual immorality; that each one of you know how to control his own body in holiness and honor, not in the passion of lust like the Gentiles who do not know God;" 1 Thessalonians 4:3-5(ESV)

"Flee from sexual immorality. Every other sin a person commits is outside the body, but the sexually immoral person sins against his own body". 1 Corinthians 6:18 (ESV)

TWO-FACED

"No servant can serve two masters, for either he will hate the one and love the other, or he will be devoted to the one and despise the other. You cannot serve God and money." Luke 16:13(ESV)

You cannot be saved just on Sundays. It just does not work. There was always tomorrow. I took for granted that I would have another chance to get it right. I would go to the club a few times a week and then go to church on Sunday. I used the same voice to praise God that I used to curse people out. I was a hypocrite, and I did not know why or how to stop. I wanted to enjoy life and be young. I felt I could get my life together once I settled down. It was hard to be two people; my heart was divided. I wanted God's love, but on my terms. I didn't want to have to stop doing what felt good to my flesh, to get what was good for my spirit. I selfishly believed that being in the world was a bigger gift than what I could receive from God. My happiness was fleeting, but I could not pinpoint why.

I honestly don't think people want to be two-faced. I think it's a lack of knowledge and understanding of what God's word says that leaves us vulnerable to constantly falling into sin cycles. We feel like it's okay just to have wine with dinner or a few drinks here and there because we're not alcoholics. Even if you are not an alcoholic, drinking alcohol has a tendency to alter our mindset and behaviors. For me, having a glass of wine reduced my inhibitions. I was more likely to send an inappropriate text to someone I swore I would never speak to again. Alcohol was like my liquid courage.

We try to explain why we can live in both worlds, but it is a difficult task to wear two faces. For instance, many people feel that it is okay to live with their significant others because they've been in a relationship for a long time, not taking into account what their decisions look like to those who look up to them. We pray for things, but also refuse to pay our tithes to the church. We get so much from our ministries and our pastors but are not willing to be obedient and give 10% to God's house. We fail to understand that all we own belongs to Him, and should be given unto Him freely.

People say that ignorance is bliss, but once we know better it is our responsibility to do better. It was exhausting for me to live two lives. What I gave up living my worldly life was nothing compared to what I gained. I received the peace and security of being in God's will for my life. I am so far from perfect, but He has healed me from some of the strongholds that hindered me from being able to live up to my full potential.

Growing Pains Life Lessons

There comes a point when you have to choose. It does not mean that you are perfect and without sin, but it does mean that you are not intentionally manipulating God's grace to live a double life. It is difficult to have friends who are not trying to walk upright and live by the commandments God has set for us. Honestly, the backlash from others can be the most difficult part of living a life for God. Many feel as though refraining from sex, drugs, and other impurities is such an unnecessary measure for salvation, not realizing that remaining pure is key to our salvation. I found that life was more difficult when I did not yield to the Holy Spirit.

Self-Reflection: Take a moment to complete the following questions

- What struggle keeps you from maturing in God?
- Take a moment to pray about an area of concern in which you struggle. Confess to God that you need His help and

strength to overcome this obstacle, and write out an action plan on how you will begin to change your actions.

Suggest Scripture(s):

"No temptation has overtaken you that is not common to man. God is faithful, and he will not let you be tempted beyond your ability, but with the temptation he will also provide the way of escape, that you may be able to endure it." 1 Corinthians 10:13 (ESV)

"Submit yourselves therefore to God. Resist the devil, and he will flee from you." James 4:7 (ESV)

HUMILITY & NOT HUMILIATION

"God resists the proud, but gives grace to the humble." James 4:6 (ESV)

I always thought of myself as a humble person. I had described myself as confident, but not conceited on numerous occasions. I took compliments wholeheartedly and always graciously said thank you. Does this not sound like the makings of a humble person? LOL Well God soon showed me that I still had some work to do when it came to the area of humility.

I was working at a University for over seven years. Unlike most jobs, resident life had a high turnover, so I saw several employees come and go. I loved what I did and really enjoyed seeing the students grow and develop over the years. For the last three years, we endured working short one or two staff members. This caused me to take on more responsibilities. Since I had been there the longest, I saw that it was naturally my responsibility, but also felt stretched.

To cushion the blow, my supervisors talked about providing a bonus as an incentive. I was happy to know that my hard work had not been in vain and that they appreciated me. I started working in both buildings, which quickly grew tiresome. The building was unorganized, and the staff was visibly frustrated. After my first week, I received the news that Human Resources had overturned the decision for my bonus, so I would not be receiving the extra pay originally agreed upon. My supervisor told me to try to negotiate other incentives, but that was to no avail. Needless to say, I was disappointed that they had not followed through on their promises.

Over the course of four to five months, I went back and forth, trained the new staff and still tried to maintain my relationship with my original building. To be honest, it was not easy, and I grew complacent. I was tired of doing two jobs, and only receiving one paycheck. To my relief, we hired someone, and I was able to relinquish my responsibilities of one of the buildings. Unfortunately, the relief did not last for long. A few months later, we found ourselves short once again. By the end of the year, I was exhausted but relieved that I had made it through the year.

I sat at our end of the year banquet in my new dress, with my hair curled and my make-up done. I listened as they called each category and announced the honorees. I applauded for my staff and co-workers as they were recognized. I was genuinely happy and excited for them until the list began to dwindle down. I soon realized that the last award had been presented, and my name had yet to be called.

I felt a wave of emotions come over me. Had there been some mistake? Was this a joke? How could I have been overlooked when I had gone above and beyond for the department? The list of responsibilities flooded my mind: taking on extra assignments, working two buildings, supervising fifteen extra staff members, teaching a course, and co-chairing several committees. Did this not warrant any recognition? I went from dismay to anger. Once again "they" had robbed me from what was mine. I spoke to my friends and a few of my co-workers about the injustice, and they agreed. They were even more outraged than I was. They had witnessed the sleepless nights and hard work I had put in.

They reassured me that my feelings were justified, and told me I deserved better. Before I could lay out the spread for my pity party, God quickly convicted me. He stopped me in my tracks. I searched my Bible for a scripture that would comfort me and found Galatians 6:9. "And let us not grow weary of doing good, for in due season we will reap, if we do not give up." I came to the harsh reality that I was constantly placing my confidence in man to reward me instead of God.

I felt short changed when I was not recognized for my "hard work", but why? I still received my paycheck and had a roof over my head. Why was this not enough? Why did I care so much about what other people thought of me? Why wasn't God's opinion of me on the forefronts of my heart and mind? Why do we allow the opinions of others to make or break us? My staff had shown me so much gratitude. The progress of my residents and the completion of another eventful school year was my gratification. It was my award.

Growing Pains Life Lesson

God used this as a teachable moment. I quickly learned that it is not always about what we think we deserve. We should always do our best, not because of what we stand to get from it, but because it is what we are called to do. Colossians 3:23-24 "Whatever you do, work heartily, as for the Lord and not for men, knowing that from the Lord you will receive the inheritance as your reward. You are serving the Lord Christ."

Self Reflection: Take a moment to answer the following questions.

- Here's a humility check. Am I more self-centered or God-centered?
- Do you find it difficult to admit you are wrong?
- Do you react when you do not receive the credit you believe you deserve?

Suggested Scripture(s):

"I appeal to you therefore, brothers, by the mercies of God, to present your bodies as a living sacrifice, holy and acceptable to God, which is your spiritual worship. Do not be conformed to this world, but be transformed by the renewal of your mind, that by testing you may discern what is the will of God, what is good and acceptable and perfect. For by the grace given to me I say to everyone among you not to think of himself more highly than he ought to think, but to think with sober judgment, each according to the measure of faith that God has assigned. For as in one body we have many members, and the members do not all have the same function, so we, though many, are one body in Christ, and individually members one of another." Romans 12:1-21(ESV)

KEEPING SECRETS AND STEALING INNOCENCE

By: Stephanie L. Randall

The birth of a baby thinking of how he's going to grow up to be an awesome man and a girl growing up to be a beautiful little lady

You pray their protection while they sleep at night reading ever Gerber food label to make sure the nutrients are right.

They look for your weakness and they stalk and prey. Nights become restless as they get more reckless not even waiting until day

Claiming that they love you and that it's your little secret, and whatever else it will take. For you not to tell and to keep it
Whatever it will take for you to not part your lips or leave a hint that you feel uncomfortable at their touch and if this is what love feels like you don't think you need it this much.

Please mommy, daddy, uncle, sister or, brother do not rob me of my innocence fore I feel I may not be able to recover.

I know that you're hurting, angry and maybe confused, and maybe you were just a child when someone did it to you.

But please I'm begging you give me a chance, the world is already going to be hard enough on me without you giving me that inappropriate glance.

Do not touch I'm fragile at heart, you're inappropriate touches are tearing me apart.

Do not satisfy this craving the enemy has implanted in you, but fight your urges and God will restore you.

God is able to heal our bruised parts and if we choose to seek him he will also renew our hearts.

KEEPING SECRETS & STEALING INNOCENCE

"One who loves his neighbor will do good, not harm. Stealing violates the law of love, because it harms our neighbor." Romans 13:9-10 (ESV)

Most people who have experienced some form of abuse in their lives have been told to keep it a secret. This protects the predator and ruins the child. The generations before us were prone to hiding what went on in their households. In turn, they embedded this idea of keeping secrets into the minds of our mothers and mothers' mothers'. I know that there can be pain in secrecy, so for my future children, I choose to walk in my truth and encourage others to do the same.

I never understood what it was about me that made men want to strip away my innocence. Was I too friendly? Was I not friendly enough? For years, I didn't understand what it was. The buildings of the Southeast apartment complex we lived in were all connected through the basement floor. As kids, we would run from building to building playing hide and seek among other games until someone's parents would kick us out, and make us play outside.

One particular day, I was playing with some friends in the downstairs laundry room when my babysitter's relative came downstairs to see what we were doing. I told him we were playing Hide and Seek. He suggested that we play Seven Minutes in Heaven instead. I had never heard of the game but thought that it was strange that he wanted to play with us. He said that it would be fun and that he would show us how to play. Most of my friends were around seven or eight, like me. He was a teenager. The other kids were excited to play. It was rare that the older kids wanted to play with us. He said that he and I would go first and show everyone how to play. He pulled me into a corner of the laundry room and unzipped his pants. I was immediately alarmed but was frozen in place. He then reached over and started to pull down my pants. I quickly told him that

I did not want to play anymore. The rest of the kids began to tease us and ran out of the laundry room leaving us alone.

He ignored their comments and told me that we would just do it for seven minutes. He began to rub his penis between my legs and moan. He was a lot taller than me, so he struggled to achieve his goal. I began to cry and scream for him to stop. He continued to hold me against the wall for what felt like an eternity before he finally let me go. I ran off, pulling up my pants along the way. I felt so scared. I ran through the tunnel to my building, up the stairs, into our apartment, and to my bedroom.

A few moments later my mother walked into my room and asked why I was running. She could see I was visibly upset and quickly asked what was wrong. I told the story to my mother, and she became angry.

"Let's go," she said as she grabbed my hand and led me out of our apartment. She marched over to the next building where my babysitter lived. We climbed to the third floor, and my mother began to bang on the apartment door. My babysitter came to the door. Before she could speak, my mother began yelling and told her what her relative had done. She also told her that he had better stay away from me or that she would deal with him herself. My babysitter was shocked. My mother did not wait for her rebuttal; she turned and headed back down the stairs as fast as we had come. When we returned home, she made sure I was okay and comforted me. My mother told me that if anyone touched me like that again that I should always tell her. I wasn't sure what happened, but I knew that it was bad. She told me what to do, but when it came time to do it I did not always follow her instructions.

Two years later, it was my next door neighbor. He was the cute fourteen-year-old brother of one of my friends. We were playing house. He was the daddy; I was the mommy. I thought that I was special because he liked me and was nice to me. I was comfortable around him. I trusted him because he was my friend's brother. Little did I know, it was not okay for him to try to kiss and hug me. He said that it was our secret.

Sometimes, the abuse does not feel wrong because we don't understand what is happening. He was cute, and I agreed to play house, so wasn't it okay? No. I was a child and did not know any better, but he should have. Since it did not feel wrong at the time, I never told my mother. I did not come to the realization of what had happened until several years later.

The U.S. Department of Health and Human Services' Children's Bureau Report Child Maltreatment 2010 found that 9.2% of victimized children were sexually assaulted.

Studies by David Finkelhor, Director of the Crimes Against Children Research Center, show that:

- 1 in 5 girls and 1 in 20 boys is a victim of child sexual abuse;

- Self-report studies show that 20% of adult females and 5-10% of adult males recall a childhood sexual assault or sexual abuse incident;

- During a one-year period in the U.S., 16% of youth ages 14 to 17 had been sexually victimized;

- Over the course of their lifetime, 28% of U.S. youth ages 14 to 17 had been sexually victimized;

- Children are most vulnerable to CSA between the ages of 7 and 13.

- According to a 2003 National Institute of Justice report, 3 out of 4 adolescents who have been sexually assaulted were victimized by someone they knew well.

Growing Pains Life Lessons

There is power in transparency and pain in secrecy. The truth shall set you free. You will not begin to heal if you compound your feelings. I encourage you as I encourage myself. Speak your truth. Pretending it never happened will not make the memories go away. You have, to be honest about your pain to be freed from the bondage. Do not continue to give them the power over your life by living in your head. God can heal our bruised places *"O Lord my God, I cried to you and you have healed me." Psalm 30:2(ESV)*

I read an article on keeping secrets, and how one family decided that they were not going to start the habit of keeping secrets. They spoke about how teaching children to be secretive could have a negative impact on them when it comes to potential child abuse. Most abusers keep children in silence and afraid by convincing them that the abuse is just a little secret. I believe that this is an important lesson to teach our children and families. It is imperative that we take preventative measures to reduce the risk of our children being preyed upon.

Look at the signs and red flags. It is your responsibility to protect your child, your brother, or sister. Every day that you stay silent is a day that someone does not get the protection they need. Do not be so consumed by your own needs that you neglect the needs of your children and family. Pay attention to your child to see if there is a change in their behavior. Be aware if they start having nightmares, shy away from someone's touch, and or start to act out. These can be signs that abuse has or is occurring. Do not trust just anyone with your children. Unfortunately, sometimes this can even mean your family and friends. Studies show that 93% of sex abuse cases are from someone that they know. If you experienced inappropriate touching from an uncle or father, do not subject your child to the people who hurt you. Be sure to break the cycle. Get the help you need so that, that spirit does not fester within you. Go to counseling, seek help from your church, and process your pain. You've been bruised, but you're not broken. You don't have to be a victim you have the power to be the Victor!

Self-Reflection: Take a moment to answer the following questions

- Have you or someone you know experienced abuse? If so, were you able to tell someone you trusted?
- How has an abusive relationship or hiding things from your past hindered your present?
- How can you help prevent abuse from happening to your children or family members?

Suggested Scripture(s):

"The thief comes only in order to steal and kill and destroy. I came that they may have and enjoy life, and have it in abundance." John 10:10 (ESV)

"Come to me, all who labor and are heavy laden, and I will give you rest. Take my yoke upon you, and learn from me, for I am gentle and lowly in heart, and you will find rest fro your souls. For my yoke is easy and my burden is light." Matthew 11:28-30 (ESV)

DAY 28

GOD, YOUR CREDIT IS GOOD WITH ME

"Jesus said to her, "I am the resurrection and the life. Whoever believes in me, though he die, yet shall he live," John 11:25 (ESV)

You know how you let a family member or friend borrow money, and they promise to pay you back, but they never do? Then a few months later they come again with the same sob story, and since you're a Christian, you have to give it to them, right? Why don't we treat God the same? Doesn't God repay us ten, a hundred, and sometimes even a thousand times fold? Shouldn't God's credit be good with us? Doesn't He continue to bless us beyond measure even when we don't deserve? If so, why do we put God in a box? Why do we short change him and give him a little credit? If we believe it and conceive it then, He will achieve it. Just because it may not be in our time does not mean that we will not bear fruit from our labor.

God wants to give us beauty for our ashes. He wants to bless us exceedingly abundantly above and beyond anything that we could ask or imagine. Are we willing to wait on Him and His timing or do we continue to try to do it on our own and pay the price? Do we not get burdened by paying the costs for our disobedience?

Although you may not have everything you want yet, God will always provide you with everything you need. I received a notice that they were increasing my student loans to an extra $100 a month. I asked for a forbearance for a month while I applied for a new loan agreement. The next month, I checked my account, and it was still too much. I felt discouraged, but I prayed and asked God to make a way for me to make the payments to keep my credit in good standing. I looked at the balance and determined that I would offer to pay $167, and ask for a payment reduction. Before I had an opportunity to call them, they called me. I explained that I wanted to make a payment, but was unable to pay the increased monthly balance.

Before I could say anything else, the rep asked me to hold while she reviewed my account. A moment later she came back to the phone and asked if she could try to qualify me for another repayment plan, and I agreed. She said that I was eligible for a plan that would make my monthly payments $167.00, and asked if that was a doable amount. I quickly agreed. I was relieved and surprised that it was the exact amount I had determined that I could pay.

That was God providing for me. She then went on to say that they would put my account into forbearance for three months and at the conclusion of that period, I would be responsible for making the first payment of $167. Now that was favor! God knew that I was trying to do the right thing and pay what I owed. Instead of having a negative attitude or feeling defeated, I trusted him to make away for me to do what I was supposed to do. I know you may be thinking who is excited about paying student loans? I am, not because I don't need that extra money in my bank account, but because I am able to pay it.

Growing Pains Life Lessons

Do we give God the opportunity to rectify our situations? We will invest six months in a dead relationship, but not invest six days in prayer and fasting to grow closer to God. I am happy that God is providing for me. I want to be a person in good standing with God and with people I have made a commitment to. My word is all I have. If people cannot trust your word, then how valuable are you to them. You appear undependable, and in genuine. There was a time when I made poor choices financially and had to rob Peter to Pay Paul as people say. Not because God was not there, but because He needed me to learn the lesson so that I would not do the same things again. I believed in God. I trusted that what He had in store for me would come to fruition. When we are in the will of God, our paths are more direct. You may not always feel his presence but, he's never far away. We just need to seek him.

Self-Reflection: Take a moment to answer the following questions

- Do you believe that God can bless you with the desires of your heart? Why or why not?
- How do you exhibit your faith in God's promises to you?

Suggested Scripture(s):

"There is therefore now no condemnation for those who are in Christ Jesus." Romans 8:1(ESV)

"Jesus said to him, "I am the way, and the truth, and the life. No one comes to the Father except through me." John 14:6 (ESV)

DAY 29

RUN YOUR RACE

"But let each one test his own work, and then his reason to boast will be in him alone and not in his neighbor." Galatians 6:4 (ESV)

When we learn to stop comparing our load to loads of those walking beside us, we can then lift the weight of the world off our shoulders. Remember the Wile E. Coyote? He kept chasing the roadrunner all over. Up and down, around and around, no matter where the roadrunner went Wile E. was on his tail. He would chase after him relentlessly, so much so that sometimes Wile E. didn't realize that the road or path that he was on had ended. The roadrunner would stop, but he would jump right off of a cliff trying to keep up with him, instead of paying attention to his own lane. Are we like that as humans? Absolutely!

I remember when I started my weight loss journey, which is a lifetime task. I started to hit the gym regularly and prided myself on exercising consistently. I would usually start off with a few miles on the treadmill to get my mojo flowing. I never liked to choose a machine right next to someone else who was working out, because I just liked to be in a zone and have my space. I would put my headphones in and get into my groove.

Sometimes, I would scan the other machines in front of me while I was working out. If I saw someone jogging while I was walking, I wanted to see what speed they were on. I was terrified of trying to run. I had seen one too many movies where someone would make one wrong step and go rolling onto the floor, lol. I started to pay attention to what type of shape the runners were in. How long had they been on the machine? I noticed that some people would have been on the treadmill for the same amount of time as I had but had already gone twice as many miles.

Once I had evaluated them, I began to wonder if they were, in turn, evaluating me. "Who was this thick chick on the treadmill?" I imagined them saying. I was clearly walking at snail's pace compared to them. The enemy used this to distract and discourage me. Should I just not work out at all? Did I just look like a joke? I quickly learned to dismiss the negative thoughts and move at my own pace. I had to do what was best for me and no one else. I learned to run my own race, and not be consumed by what the next person was doing.

I've had so many students talk to me about what their hopes and dreams are but, in the same breath, tell me that they are not able to pursue their passions because of family pressures. Sometimes those pressures come from dealing with family members who did not feel higher education was important. In their selfishness, they then downplay what their student was trying to achieve. On the other end of the spectrum were the students whose parents were very supportive, but only to a certain extent. Their parents wanted to live vicariously through them encouraging them to achieve what they had not been able to.

My response was always the same. You have to live for you! We want to seek wise counsel from our parents and families, but we ultimately have to make a decision based on what is best for us. If we fail to do that, we can end up resentful and unhappy.

Growing Pains Life Lessons

I'm sure that you have heard people say that they are just "in their own lane." That is a great place to be. When we began to look over at others, it distracts us from our own journey. So many times we compare ourselves to those around us. We are so consumed by what they are doing that we can't get anything done ourselves. If we are uncertain of what direction to go in, we can always look up. We cannot live for or through others, but instead we must be content with what God's will is for us. Do not allow other's opinions to derail what God has said to you.

Self-Reflection: Take a moment to answer the following questions.

- In what ways have you chosen to live for others?
- How can comparison hinder you from achieving your goals?
- How have other people's opinions of you dictated your decisions?

Suggested Scripture(s):

"You're blessed when you stay on course, walking steadily on the road revealed by God. You're blessed when you follow his directions, doing your best to find him. That's right - you don't go off on your own; you walk straight along the road he set. You, God, prescribed the right way to live; now you expect us to live it. Oh, that my steps might be steady, keeping to the course you set; Then I'd never have any regrets in comparing my life with your counsel. I thank you for speaking straight from your heart; I learn the pattern of your righteous ways. I'm going to do what

you tell me to do; don't ever walk off and leave me." Psalm 119:1-8 (ESV)

DAY 30

DON'T GET LOST IN THE LESSON

"For the righteous falls seven times and rises again, but the wicked stumble in times of calamity." Proverbs 24:16 (ESV)

One night when I was about six-years-old, I went into the kitchen and noticed that the stove was still on. I was fascinated by the fire, so I grabbed my paper towel and held it to the flame. The paper towel quickly became engulfed in the flames. I began to panic as the fire grew closer to my tiny fingers. I quickly waved the disintegrating fabric back and forth to no avail. I did the only sensible thing… I threw the fire-ridden paper towel into the trashcan. I felt a sigh of relief as I quickly scattered down the hall and into my bedroom. I tucked myself in and sank into my pillow. Moments later, my bedroom lights flicked on, and I saw my mother standing in the doorway with an angry look on her face. She asked what had I put in the trash can. I got nervous and quickly said that I had put my trash in the bathroom trash can. I knew how to lie, but I surely was not good at it. My mother marched me to the bathroom and told me to show her. I went over to the wastebasket, but to my dismay there was not a piece of paper in sight, and most importantly not my napkin! Needless to say I got a serious whooping. At the time, I thought that I was spanked because I lied. I did not understand the magnitude of my actions, or what the true lesson was. I did not realize the bigger picture of my actions. Not only had I lied, but I had played with fire, which could have killed us if my mother had not caught it in time.

How many times have you failed to consider the magnitude of your actions? I had an employee who was about 19-20 years old. She was friendly and had done a great job for the month and a half that she had been working for me. One day, I gave her instructions to do something and she quickly rebutted, "I'm not doing that!" I was kind of shocked and even more irritated. It had been a long day, and I was in no mood to argue with her. Anyone who knows me knows that I really do not like to repeat myself, and on top of that, I really did not like staff telling me what they were not going to do. I told her she would do what I asked or that she could go home for the rest of the day. She huffed and went on to complete the task.

A week later, she came to work and had three friends with her. I immediately asked her what the policy was for bringing friends to work. She said she usually had friends come with her and did not see the problem. Her attitude was poor, and I was over going back and forth with her. I called her into my office to have a meeting with her. I explained to her that I thought our communication had been off the last two weeks, and I really was not pleased with her demeanor when I addressed my concerns about her job performance and attitude.

She sat in front of me, rolled her eyes and became upset. She said she did everything I asked of her, and she was not sure why she was getting "yelled at" I was confused by her tone and told her I was not yelling at her; however, I was trying to address her inappropriate behavior. I explained to her that if she worked at a law firm, she would not be able to mosey on in with her crew and hang out.

"I am trying to teach you how to establish a professional rapport," I continued hoping that she was grasping what I was saying. Then she did the unexpected. . . she began to cry! It seemed like a joke, almost like a hidden camera show. I was surprised by her sudden change of emotions. She said she did not understand why I was telling her she was not doing a good job when she did everything I asked her to do.

I quickly brought back to her remembrance the last two weeks, but it fell on deaf ears. She just kept saying she did not understand. Now the issue was not that she did not understand, but that she did not want to. She wanted to keep up with the illusion that she was being mistreated, and that I was being "mean to her". She could not focus on what she was doing wrong or the feedback I was trying to give her.

She could only see what was happening to her and not what I was trying to do for her. I suggested that she reread her handbook and think about what I had said. I told her she could return to work and I sat in my office dumbfounded, almost ready to break out in laughter from the ridiculousness of it all.

I was astonished at how she had responded. She quickly got lost in the lesson. She overlooked everything I said and focused on what she wanted to hear. She acted out of emotion and not logic.

Growing Pains Life Lessons

Does this sound familiar? When God does not allow you to get your way immediately, do you pout and cry? Or, do you realize that He may have a bigger purpose and plan He is trying to get you to see? Do you strive to listen or close your ears to

His voice? I urge you to not get so caught up in the "no" that you miss Him trying to show you how to experience the yes.

We need to be honest when we label things as a mistake. A mistake is an unconscious action. A decision is an intentional action. Once a mistake is repeated, it becomes a decision. We should not keep allowing ourselves to escape the responsibility of our decisions by calling them mistakes. Instead, we should take the corrective action to learn from our mistakes and stop making poor decisions. I have learned time and time again that if we fail the lesson God has for us the first time, we will have to continue to take it over and over until we get it right. It may not always manifest itself the same way each time, but the underlying lesson is always the same

Self-Reflection: Take a moment to answer the following questions.

- What lesson are you continuously failing?
- What is keeping you from making the necessary changes?
- How would a change in your behavior yield better results?

Suggested Scripture(s):

"Now these things happened to them as an example, but they were written down for our instruction, on whom the end of the ages has come." 1 Corinthians 10:11 (ESV)

NOT BUILT TO BREAK

"We are afflicted in every way, but not crushed; perplexed, but not driven to despair; persecuted, but not forsaken; struck down, but not destroyed; always carrying in the body the death of Jesus, so that the life of Jesus may also be manifested in our bodies" 2 Corinthians 4:8-10 (ESV)

Have you ever wondered why you have had to endure so much over your life? I sometimes compared my life to a soap opera. As soon as I put out one fire in my life, another one was quickly burning. I considered myself a "good person." I was a child of God, so why did I have to go through so much. I began to have a different attitude about obstacles that sprung up in my life. I learned that I would have seasons of my life that would test my faith. By seasons, I am not referring to winter, spring, summer, and fall. I am referring to the seasons of life circumstances.

There were seasons in which I had an abundance of money and wanted for nothing, but then there was a season of my life in which things were tight. I had taken an extreme pay cut, and I did not have the funds to keep up the life I was accustomed to. I had to use my credit cards to pay for monthly bills I could no longer afford. I felt relieved until I had racked up thousands of dollars in debt I could not pay. It took me almost five years to pay off my debt and rebuild my credit. It was difficult not to go on vacations with everyone else, or buy expensive bags. I was a college graduate, intelligent and hardworking, but the poor choices I made derailed me.

I often asked, "God, why didn't you stop me or give me a sign that I was going in the wrong direction?" God will only put on us what He knows we can bear. Even when we feel like we're going to crumble, He knows our strengths and our weaknesses. He knows what we're going to do before we do it. Will He stop us? No, that's why he gave us free will. "The heart of man plans his way, but the Lord establishes his steps." Proverbs 16:9 God wants us to exhibit our faith in him. It is not for us to do on our own. He should be the source of our strength. Take your hands off the things that you cannot control. *"I can do all things through him who strengthens me." Philippians 4:13 (ESV)*.

My senior year of high school, I only applied to two universities: Bowie State University and University of Maryland Eastern Shore. I received an acceptance letter from UMES, as well as a partial scholarship. I was excited to go to culinary school and start the next part of my life. My fairytale was quickly brought to a halt when my mother announced that she did not want me to go to Eastern Shore because it was a "party school." I was upset and in total disbelief that my mother would not allow me to go. I was only seventeen at the time, so I had to have her signature to enroll.

My mother decided to send me to Bowie State, but there was a surprise for both of us. . .I was not accepted! I was an honor roll student with a 3.1 GPA, but I had been denied. We later found out I was a few points short on my SATs, and would have to retake them to achieve a higher score for acceptance. I was devastated. I had missed out on my opportunity to go to my dream school and now had been rejected from my backup. I was heartbroken. Only two people in my immediate family had gone to college and were both unable to finish. They expected me to be the first, and I did not want to let them or myself down.

Acting off of my emotions, I decided that if I could not go to Eastern Shore, I would not go anywhere! I obtained a full-time job at a Real Estate company, and two part-time jobs to make ends meet. Three months after my 18th birthday, I moved into my own place with a roommate (you already know how that ended, lol). I enjoyed working and being on my own, but there was still a void. I knew that I needed to go to college. A year went by, and I decided to apply to UMES again, and was accepted! I was beyond grateful for the chance and decided I would go no matter what.

In the spring of 2002, I became a college student. I loved the experiences, education, and relationships I built. I worked hard and graduated in 3.5 years with a job offer in one hand and keys to a house in the other. I overcame! I knew what God had built me to do, and I knew it would happen. It didn't happen when and how I thought, but the most important thing is that it did!

Growing Pains Lessons

Take heed to my experience. Believe that although it may seem difficult, God can give you the strength and the grace to achieve your heart's desires. God wants us to prosper; He does not set us up to fail. We need to take back our power. Know that when it feels like everything is closing in on you, it's only a test. Will you bend or will you break? Once the enemy sees your weakness, he will continue to use that against you. When that stops working, they will switch it up and try something else.

Make up in your mind that you are going to come out of every situation and season victorious. Sometimes, that victory may be learning how to cope, or how to deal with situations with grace. God did not sacrifice His only son for us to perish. He wants us to live life abundantly. Don't get discouraged in the face of adversity. This journey has been amazing, but it does not stop here. I am now and always will be a work in progress. I may get knocked down, but God will never count me out. He will be with me in the midst of every season, encouraging me and keeping me through all my growing pains.

Self-Reflection: Take a moment to answer the following questions.

- What is a desire of your heart that you want God to bring to fruition?
- How can you S.L.A.Y. the obstacles that will come your way?

Suggested Scripture(s):

"And there appeared to him an angel from heaven, strengthening him." Luke 22:43 (ESV)

Let's Connect

For bookings, group book rates, and events please email me at mydivineopportunity@gmail.com. Please include your name, contact number, and date of the event.

Follow me on Facebook at: My Divine Opportunity, LLC

Follow me on Instagram at: Msworththewait

Tweet me at: Msworththewait

www.ingramcontent.com/pod-product-compliance
Lightning Source LLC
Chambersburg PA
CBHW080337170426
43194CB00014B/2604